Horses Have Wings

Memoirs of a Horse Listener

Peter Van Minnen

ISBN 978-0-9559925-0-6 PUBLISHED BY LULU.COM
COPYRIGHT: HORSES HAVE WINGS
BY PETER VAN MINNEN 2008

Dedication

This book is dedicated to my many teachers, in this life

and those that have gone before.

Among them:

My Dear Parents, Ernie and Ethne,

Mentors

Ewald and Gail Meggersee, Sheila Toms,

My Friend Linda Scott, who was instrumental in calling

me to this work,

My Beloved Soulmate, Debra, who constantly inspires

me and encourages me, and, of course, the many Horses,

My Brothers and Sisters, My Friends,

Manifest and Unmanifest,

Mentioned and unmentioned in this book,

Who are my true Teachers.

Also:

To the White Horse, my friend and guide.

To All That Is.

"If I don't go within,
I go without…"(Anon.)

CONTENTS

ix

Krumpet: 18-04-06

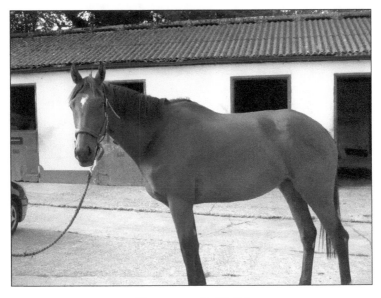

Krumpet: 5-08-06

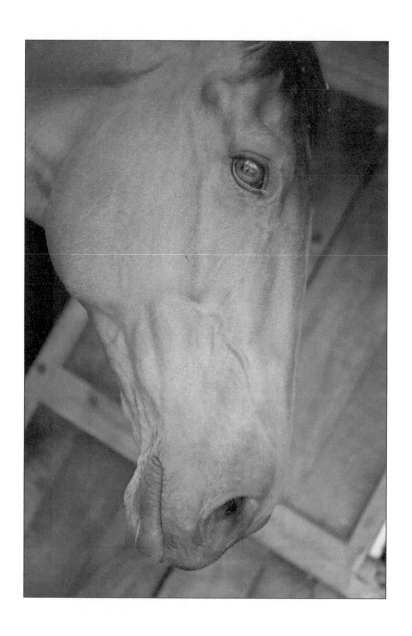

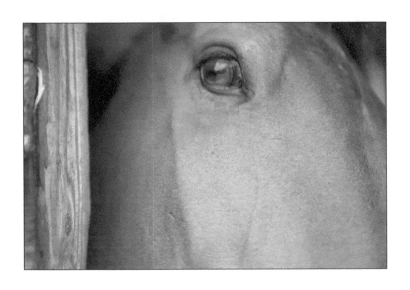

Photographs courtesy of Marie Stone

Introduction: *Intuition and 'Listening'*

It has taken a while for me to decide to write this
book.

One reason for this delay is the difficulty in finding
the appropriate vocabulary, the language to describe
the work I do.

I believe it is a subtle art, much of it feels instinctive,
as if it's something I learnt from a time before. Some
of it is technique-based; there are aspects of healing,
acupressure, energy/chakra balancing, and even an
adapted version of the technique called Body Stress
Release, which I have practiced on human beings over
the last 14 years.

In addition to this I make no apologies for borrowing
from others, many of these being masters at what they
do:

It is said that there is nothing new under the sun, and
that we already have everything we need, that we
know everything from the moment that we are born. It
is then just a matter of remembering what we have
forgotten…Every teacher we meet on our life-journey
reminds us, brings out that knowledge.

However, the way in which each individual expresses his or her gift is unique, even though they may seem, at first, to be coming from the same place.

On many occasions people have asked me whilst I have been treating their horses,
"What are you actually doing?"
On almost as many occasions I have been unable to answer them to their complete satisfaction!

So this book is an attempt to make things clearer, both to others and myself.
I may, therefore, from time to time, be creating a vocabulary to assist you, the reader, in grasping the often-intuitive nature of the Work.
What then is *'intuitive'*?
What does it really mean?
And are all people *'intuitive'*, or only some?
If all people are intuitive, why doesn't everyone feel what I feel, see what I see?
I can't answer that with any certainty, but I shall make an attempt to explain things as I see them.
I believe that women are, by nature, intuitive, and it is not therefore, surprising that most of the people I meet

in my work with horses are women, who instinctively find what I do acceptable, if perhaps a little weird. Still, on some level, they *'get it'*....

Perhaps this is because, at the level of intuition, there is an understanding, a connectedness, which is universal, *which crosses the divide between the species: a kind of wordless language spoken by every stone, plant and creature on the planet.*
This 'language' is accessible to all, if one is open to it...

So here it is, my idea of what *Intuition* is:
Every day, all day and at every moment, there are those voices, words, images that quietly offer us guidance and advice; suggesting without compulsion, showing without forcing.

These are signposts from the inner self, I believe, which still leave us completely free to choose which path to take.

God's voice, if you will.

For example, someone you have not seen or heard of for ages suddenly enters your thoughts, pops into your head.

Later, it may even be the same day; that very person phones you or you walk into them in the street...

We've all had this, haven't we? In some form or another.

This is Intuition.

All people have it.

All the time.

Few heed it or take any notice of it.

There are some who say this intuitive voice comes from our *'feminine side'* or right brain, distinct from our *'masculine side',* which is the everyday left brain attuned to waking reality. This left brain is more intellectual, scientific, fragmented....

The left brain sees details, the parts: it is analytical, masculine

The right brain sees the whole picture: it is intuitive, feminine.

Intuition is the inspirational everyday language of Artists, Poets, Playwrights and Innovators.

Creative types.

(Don't feel left out! Everyone, I believe, has a creative side!)

Einstein admitted to being deeply indebted to the power of intuition and he was, nonetheless, a scientist!

It seems that when we are one with the *Flow* of life, in harmony with ourselves and the Universe, we *automatically* become more intuitive, we might say *'in tune with it'*, to play on the word a little…

We then see the world for what it truly is, a great interconnected living Being, with every single part knowing the Unity of the Whole, no part really separate from any other, nor ever having been so.

One.

What sociologists and psychologists seem to be saying today is that the sickness of our time is separateness, loneliness.

We feel we are alone, isolated from one another, cut off from Source…many even denying Its existence.

But are we really,

Are we ever, completely alone?

Some say we are never alone. That we are always assisted, protected even, by *'guides' or 'guardian angels',* Helpful spirits, always with us, waiting to be asked to assist us, which they surely will do, but only when called upon to do so. This is, I am told, because of their respect for human free will…

So it may well be that we are surrounded on all sides, inside and outside of us by many orders of helpful higher beings on many dimensional levels.

In the words of William Shakespeare: *'there are more things in heaven and earth than are dreamed of in your philosophy...'*

One can find, without looking too hard, many descriptions, often by clairvoyants or psychics, of nature-spirits, sometimes called *fairies*, *elementals* or *devas* working within the processes of Nature, watching over the progress of humans, animals and plants on the Earth...

Perhaps it is just because we cannot see them that we imagine ourselves to be alone, I rather suspect that this is the case.

But what we imagine has great power over us, for better or worse,

We create our world in this way, positively or negatively, by way of what we imagine, what we project out through our feelings and thoughts, from within ourselves.

Intuition reminds us of our unity, our *Oneness* with all things.

It reminds us that others, perhaps thousands of miles away, are only ever a thought away, therefore never far away at all.

Intuition reminds us that even those that we believe are gone, through Death, Are always with us, and not just through our memories.

Our ancestors, past, are constantly watching over us, shaping things, even now, in this Eternal Present.

Intuition reminds us that we are always far greater than we believe ourselves to be, and that all things are always possible.

This, I should also add, though it sounds vaguely mystical, is exact and precise *intuitive* knowledge, free of the divisive influence of the intellect, useful as that may be in the physical world of matter.

Mozart described receiving musical inspiration as a "Single Moment". Everything, an entire Symphony received in that one instant! His musical scores are never corrected, they are intact and a Unity.

This is the way of Intuition, single, undivided.

There is a Lakota saying: *'HOONKAPI'* meaning:
'We are all related'

This is the spirit in which I write this book.

7

Let's enjoy it, together!

I hope that this book will also be entertaining, life can be all too serious sometimes, and perhaps we could all do with a little lightening up.

Perhaps even a good laugh!

Recently it has been proven that when we laugh the body releases benign chemicals called endorphins, which actually heal the cells and boost the immune system...

Chapter One: *Our Friends the Horses.*

This book would not be complete without some kind of dedication to our friends the horses, and the incredible debt we owe them.

According to The Institute for Ancient Equestrian Studies, recent archaeological research has discovered evidence of bit wear on the teeth of horses dated to 3500BC in Kazakhstan, (which pushes back the beginning of horse riding 1500 years earlier than was previously supposed by historians)

There are ancient Babylonian reliefs showing horses in harness and Bronze Age chariots have been found buried in tombs on the Steppes of Russia. Proof enough of the long service of horses in harness.

The domestication of horses *per se* preceded this by several thousand years.

Apparently they were herded and used for meat and milk, long before thought was applied to the riding of them…

More recently they have been used as beasts of burden, taking explorers and their baggage deep into mountains and inaccessible places, never complaining or shirking their duties.

They have been employed as war-horses, plunging courageously into the thick of battle, suffering unspeakable injury, mutilation and death.
All of it in utter willingness and dedication to their riders, never questioning their motives and intentions, as suicidal and pointless as these often were…
And who has mourned them, who has spoken their epitaph……?
I remember seeing profoundly disturbing photographs of piles of dead horses on the Western Front, slaughtered in the conflicts of the First World War. There must have been hundreds, if not thousands that gave their lives in the course of what seemed to be a shockingly pointless loss of life.
In short, the history of the western world is inconceivable without the horse.

But, in spite of this debt we owe, we see few monuments to the horses that have served us so bravely. (One exception being the recently –unveiled memorial to the animals near Hyde Park.)

However, we do see tapestries, which chronicle the great battles and quests of the Middle Ages, featuring armed men on horseback.

We see the medieval tapestry: *'The Lady and the Unicorn'* raising the horse to the level of the Mythical and the Mystical, as we see also with Pegasus the winged horse, much earlier in ancient Greece.

No other animal in the history of the western world has been elevated to this level of respect.

(I have made mention of Pegasus in the chapter entitled "Horses have Wings".)

We see the great pre-Christian bronze horses of St.Mark's in Venice, and we hear that Leonardo Da Vinci attempted to cast the largest-ever statue of a horse.

Sadly it did not survive the casting.

Everywhere, in fact, we testify to the beauty of the horse in our Art.

But still, there are not many places where we have shown our gratitude.

I have always been a great admirer of the Native
American culture, or what remains of it. These are
people who have always respected the horse, even
creating new breeds from the horses left there by the
Spaniards.
Their horsemanship can teach us much about listening
to the horse, about tuning-in to it, riding with
awareness so that we mentally connect with it, so that
horse and rider are **One**......

Perhaps we are about to move into more enlightened
times,
Where we can show this beautiful animal the respect
it deserves.
There are some who are already showing the way,
people like Monty Roberts,
Who has discovered the language, the body language
of horses, which he calls *'Equus'*, this through his
having lived with mustangs in the wild.

This is a man who travels the world sharing his
secrets, and who has done much to make the training
of horses more gentle and humane, more effective,
even finding ways to overcome behavioural problems,

the principles of which he now applies to delinquent teenagers.

Perhaps his books should be essential reading to all of those involved in the training of horses.
There are many others like Monty Roberts, many who are doing good work for our friends the horses.
For indeed: we ought to see them as our friends.
They have carried us, stood by us, saved us from harm,
Needing little from us in return and always willing to go that extra mile.
As loyal as any friend and as faithful.
And when a friend is in need, do we not respond and help him?
And when a friend calls out for help, do we not listen?

This book is about *'listening'*
Or my idea of what that is,
My way of listening.
There are other ways,
Many.
This is just one of the many.

"We have two ears but only one mouth, therefore we should listen twice as much as we speak...."

Chief Seattle.

Chapter Two: *About Me and How I Started Out.*

I grew up in what was then a tiny fishing village on
the Cape coast called Hermanus, now a world-famous
whale-watching mecca, some eighty miles south of
Cape Town.

Seeing the (*'southern right'*) whales in Walker Bay
spouting, fluking, feeding their young, hearing them
call to each other was, for me, a part of growing up.
So was living in on and around the sea.

Hardly a day went by when we were not playing in
the waves, running on the beaches, digging in the sand
looking for mussels, or just scanning the sea for
porpoises, which would leap playfully in the breakers.
These were days measured by endless summer
sunshine, the caress of the sea as we surfed the
sparkling waves, and our constant curiosity over the
sea's inhabitants; in rock pools, on the beach, at the
harbour.

Since my childhood I have been back to this place
many times and it has not lost any of its charm. It is
still special, magical.

My father was a *perlemoen* (*abalone*) diver then, spending most of his days in or under the sea when the weather permitted it, and on wintry days when the sea was too rough to dive; repairing and selling radios and hi-fi systems in his shop, which was called *'Minnen's Radio Service'*.

Back then TV had not yet arrived and radio was all we had to entertain us.

I remember the smell of burnt solder and hot radio valves, and the sparky, hissy sounds of radio-sets being tuned in, restored and repaired.

It was a dangerous place where we children kept a respectful distance!

For me, at that time, my dad was this awesome person who was actually several people: one day he was a diver, emerging like a god from the depths of the sea swathed in a wet black rubber diving suit, face hidden behind a diving mask, on another day he was a radio engineer, with dials and instruments and soldering iron orchestrating and taming electrical chaos into orderly sounds and voices emerging from radio sets. To me he was all-powerful, all-knowing and magical to be around.

To him I owe my love for music, especially classical music, which he would love to listen to at full volume, on hi-fi systems he had built himself.

He had been an enthusiast since his childhood, building his first radio set whilst still at school.

He was also a natural clown, to me, the funniest man I have ever known.

He taught me to find humour in everything, that laughter overcomes gravity, and that laughter can even heal where nothing else will....

There was never a dull moment in our home, and I was never, ever bored!

Though I know times were often hard for my parents, this was a wonderful childhood for me, one in which it could be truly said that there was a constant communion with Nature and her forces.

My father would watch the sea and the weather from the cliff tops for a long long time before considering the risks of taking his boat and crew out on the waves.

First thing in the morning I would hear him tapping the glass dial on the barometer, which was another essential ritual to be observed before going out to the cliff tops.

At times we would be made more acutely aware of the dangers of the sea.

In winter we would go down to the cliffs, following a furious storm, to see trawlers wrecked by the heavy seas, reduced to pieces of timber and floating debris.

From early childhood I can remember seeing the body of a diver lying on our kitchen floor, (whether he was alive or dead was unknown to me at the time), seawater and seaweed all around him…me hiding away, peering around the kitchen door and not noticed in the chaos and panic of the attempts to revive the poor soul…

At other, lighter, times we would love to body surf the sparkling waves which cascaded onto the beautiful long white beaches, often accompanied by friendly porpoises.

It was a magical place to grow up into the world.

It felt safe; people in the village were friendly and caring.

Truly, my own kind of paradise.

Then, when I was around 11 or 12 years old, we left Hermanus and moved to Cape Town. This was an exciting time for us children, even though we had left our paradise. To us, this was now *the big city*, a place of wonders!

Buses, trains, department stores! Sights and sounds we had never known before...

People wore shoes and suits; it was a busy bustling place full of dark secrets and bright dreams, danger and magic happening all at once...

My father took a job in a big hi-fi and radio shop in the city and we boys went to school in a far more ordered and exclusive setting than the little village school, where we had been used to seeing boys arriving in the morning on tractors, and where very few of us even wore shoes.

Now, we travelled to school on great big double-decker buses and wore uniforms! This was cool!

It was all new and exciting and at first we didn't miss Hermanus at all....

So then came six years in High School and with it, lots of wonderful new friends. At around sixteen years of age I worked as a kind of apprentice in the studio of an architect, who was a friend of my Dad's. I got to really like it and decided then and there that it was just what I wanted :I was going to become an *Architect!*

On finishing school, and a further probationary period of two years working for architects, to get the feel of things, I entered University to study Architecture and then before you can say *'t-square'*, I was salaried in an architect's office.

I loved it, I had always loved art and creativity and now I was creating and drawing, designing houses and buildings:

Real things in the real world that had begun life as ideas.

It was my mother who encouraged my artistic side. She has a natural ability for drawing and painting, and loves putting her hand to anything creative. She taught me to draw and paint, to love beautiful things and to appreciate Art.

She would throw herself into "helping" us in school themes and projects which required artwork, often doing most of it herself!

So, after some years in the practice of Architecture, in a career that spanned many different kinds of projects, and which was often exciting and enjoyable,

I quite suddenly made the decision to give up
Architecture, in order to study and practice Body
Stress Release. *Something was calling me.*

I had suffered a bad back for years, at last found
lasting relief in Body Stress Release, or BSR. As
destiny would have it, I had been made redundant
twice in the space of eighteen months, this after a
career spanning around fifteen years, in which I had
always found work. So I decided then and there to
quit the drawing board and to retrain as a BSR
practitioner in order to help out people with bad
backs! *Something had been calling me for a while.*
Part of me had always been drawn to healing and I
suspected that I had some natural ability for it.

So, fast forward two years later, and now here I was,
living in England and making a new life for myself.
I had been practicing the Body Stress Release
technique for around four years, in February 1996,
when I got a call from my friend Linda.
She and I met a couple a years before, when she
brought her husband Roy to my rooms so that I could
treat his shoulder problem.

Although BSR is a technique, which though gentle
and non-manipulative, is physical and based on
triggering healing responses from the body in order to
release tension which has become locked into the
muscles, and which anyone can train to do,
Linda somehow saw my potential as a healer straight
off.
She described cones of light, of many colours, all
around me, as I was working on Roy.

I remember that she also asked me if I was interested
in treating horses.
I told her that I had applied BSR to dogs, but not
horses.
Now, I shall make no attempt to hide the fact that I am
aware that I have been given a gift, and that this gift is
there, I believe to help others, and comes from the
Beyondness…

I should also mention that in 1992 I spent several
months training with a healer in South Africa,
learning to use these gifts, becoming sensitized,
opening up to Spirit, under the watchful eye of a
wonderfully gifted woman called Sheila Toms, who

had developed her healing ways through a crisis in her personal life.

A number of, at times, life-threatening allergies and food-sensitivities, had struck her daughter over a period of years.

So Sheila had to learn fast, as there was not much information or mainstream help available for the things that were threatening her daughter's fragile health.

She had learned to dowse, to become intuitive at every level, to trust her feelings for what was the right treatment, the right foods, the appropriate action.

I am told that Spirit often works in this way, opening us up to our gifts and encouraging us in often surprising ways, often through illness or crises like Sheila's.

Her story is one which should be told, it would encourage and give hope to many, but this book is about horses, and here I shall leave off, not forgetting to honour Sheila for opening up for me the eyes of Spirit, for her teachings.

So my friend Linda phoned me up one day, and this is pretty much what she said:

'My daughter's horse Lizzie is not well.

She is lame.

We have had the vet round. He has had her on anti-inflammatory medications for some time now, but it's made no difference. She is still lame.

You came into my mind whilst I was here with Lizzie. Then, later on, when I was meditating at home, Spirit confirmed this again:

It would be right for you to see Lizzie, it will be your introduction to horses.

This is what Spirit have to say to you, this will be your start....'

So I immediately agreed to see Lizzie, who was I to argue with Spirit!

It was the 23rd February 1996. I remember it being a cold winter's day.

I was a bit nervous, I had never treated a horse before, although we had briefly covered the treatment of animals during the Body Stress Release course, and were shown how we could adapt BSR to work on them, given the variation in the number of vertebrae

in the lumbar area between humans and other
mammals.

I knew, though, as I laid hands on Lizzie, that this was
more than just the application of BSR training.
I could feel a surge of energy running through the
mare, through my hands.
It was as if my hands had become a conduit, a
channel for energy. A kind of electrical 'flow-system'.
Oddly enough, the mare was not disturbed by it.
In fact, she soon relaxed altogether, her neck
drooping, along with mouth and lips.
With her eyes closed, she even seemed asleep.
I felt 'directed' to placing my left hand on her withers,
at the root of the neck, and the other hand to her
lumbar/sacral spine.
I also applied, very gently, the BSR technique, as far
as possible, on the muscles along the spine; using
only a minimum of pressure, and noticed her response
to it,
The two things seemed to complement each other, the
energies of what I would come to recognize as natural
healing, combined with BSR.

With this first session on a horse, I was aware only that something instinctive and powerful was helping *Lizzie*, and I was glad to be a part of it!

I saw her again a week later, she was already a lot better, I was told.

Then again, two weeks after that, when there was the sense that she was well on the way to recovery, the lameness was gone, she had come back to herself…

I treated *Lizzie* twice more, based on what I felt intuitively was appropriate, around a month later each time.

It was interesting to see that there were moments when she went through a kind of *'healing crisis'* after a session, things seemed worse with her for a day or two. But then a day came when she did not need any more help…

She was healed!

This was great!

I loved being around horses; it seemed so natural to me, as if I had always done it, as if I was born to do it…

After *Lizzie*, my phone just kept ringing.

People in the yard where I had treated her, saw her recovery first-hand, and wanted some of this for their own horses.

And so the word spread.
And so it was that I was launched into the world of *Horse Listening*, as I later came to describe it
Of course, the animals themselves have taught me a lot, and I have added tools to assist the process, things I have learned and studied over the years.
These include aspects of *acupressure, energy psychology/tapping and re-connective healing.*
I begin gradually to *'see'* things more clearly as time goes on, always trusting the information, always knowing that this is a partnership, between the horse and myself or between me and any other animal, a cooperation in healing.
It helps that I love animals, that I respect them and have a natural empathy with them.

I am disinclined to see them as inferior beings to us humans, most certainly there are differences between us, but what unites us is the air we breathe, and, of course, **Love**...

In all humility, I do not know, when I begin work, what will happen next, or in what way information will come to me.

Sometimes I see and feel things, sometimes not.

Sometimes I lay my hands on a horse and *step away, allowing Spirit to work through me.*

However, every time I lay my hands on a horse, I pray.

I ask Spirit to help me, to work through me, to allow healing to take place, to facilitate healing through me.

I know that in this way the circle is complete,

And in Truth,

That we are **One**.

There are techniques for developing the 'eyes of spirit', for bringing more clarity into these intuitive abilities.

Obviously, the clearer one is about oneself and within oneself, the clearer the picture of what one is seeing.

Even at the best of times, this vision is *'through a glass darkly'*, meaning that all is coloured by one's own perceptions, one's own limitations.

I will touch on these things throughout the book; they are useful in describing the means to sharpen one's intuitive skills.

I have found meditation to be the most powerful tool
for refining inner vision;
For strengthening *'spiritual muscle',* for creating inner
stillness and peace.
What kind of meditation, you may ask?
It really doesn't matter; there are many kinds to suit
all tastes.
I have been practicing meditation since the age of
seventeen,
Not always as regularly as I would like to, but it has
certainly brought inner calm and security into my life,
Proving the truth of the ancient adage:
'If I don't go within, I go without'

Chapter Three: *Why 'Horse Listener'?*

So why do I call myself a *'Horse Listener?'*

By now, through my attempts to define the nature of intuition, you would be getting an idea of why I chose the word *'Listener'*.

Because Intuition is just that: a kind of listening. I shall elaborate:

Traditionally, there is a long and ancient line of peculiarly gifted persons respected for their inward, intuitive ability to communicate *spiritually* with horses (and usually other creatures). In the past they were often called shamans, or in some cultures, medicine men or women.

So this means that there was and is, a communication between this person and *the spirit of* the horse, in a way, a transfer of information between one species and another, at a profoundly deep level: *The language of the Soul.*

Small wonder they are held in such awe, since most of us long for this long-lost ability, one we had, according to legend, before the tower of Babel.

Also, and in addition to this, there are clearly some trainers who have something of this ability in their work;

Displaying a direct communication and cooperation with the horse.

Amongst them Monty Roberts stands out head and shoulders.

I have seen him at work and it is stirring and heart-warming stuff to see.

Monty has spent his entire life with horses and he points out in his books that there is a language horses use, a body language that he refers to as *'Equus'*.

He deciphered this language by spending long hours with mustangs in the wild, watching their every move, noticing for instance how the dominant mare drive unruly youngsters out of the protective herd, where they are susceptible to the attention of predators! Only when they show themselves to be submissive and willing to cooperate are they allowed back into the safe protection of the herd. This is a key element in Monty's work: the discovery that the horse is a social animal, craving approval from the leader, and willing always to submit to that leader.

Distinctly apart from those involved, like Monty Roberts, in the training and management of horses, there is another group altogether different, yet related.

This is the group of highly gifted Intuitive healers I mentioned earlier, who call themselves *'Horse Whisperers'*. Most of them have the ability to know instantly what horses are thinking and feeling, often in a highly detailed and accurate way.
Clearly this is happening at a level other than the physical, beyond body language, beyond what we apprehend with the five senses.
This is at the level of the soul.

At this level, some *Whisperers* even claim to be able to access the past lives of horses. Some, and I personally know of at least one of these, can communicate with horses from afar, often via a photograph of that animal.
The person I know of has been able to provide amazingly detailed information about what the horse prefers to eat, what it thinks about its home and the other horses, and even what it feels about its owner!
Useful stuff;

Showing the evolutionary emergence of personality in the horse kingdom.

There are others, who are even able to use their gifts and abilities to diagnose,

To pinpoint problems and diseases in the horse, sometimes overlooked by the vet. This can, of course, lead to some conflict of professional interest, even a clash of egos!

At the end of it all, though, we are all of us, at heart, simply trying to help that horse, so beloved of its owner,

Who just wants to see it well and happy again,

Even if it means trying another road to get to that place of Healing..

I have chosen to call myself a *Horse Listener* because this is what I do.

I listen,

I tune in:

I tune in

To the body and to the Soul.

I access information, which is given at all kinds of levels,

It is a kind of language,

To which I *listen*,

And *listening in inner stillness* is required in order to access this information.

Information can come from the state of the muscles,

They can tell me if they are tense or spasmed,

And how this will affect the animal's ability to move, to coordinate.

Information can come from the cellular memory of that animal, in a very detailed way, which might describe past trauma or injury (described later in the book) trapped in the cells- *the body remembers physical, mental or emotional trauma.*

Other kinds of information are provided at other levels,

All of this through what I call *Listening.*

Over the years, there have been those who have referred to me as a *Horse Whisperer*, and I do not have a problem with this,

However there are those who call themselves *Whisperers*, whereas they are, in fact, gifted trainers, not healers.

This confuses things.

It is for this reason that I have decided, for the sake of accuracy, to call myself a *'Horse Listener'*, that is: one who *'Listens'*, or *tunes in*, to horses.
It could be said, if one is looking for a definition of this capitalised version of the word:

'Listening is the active inner process of a faculty called Intuition'

Chapter Four: *Feeling Safe.*

When pain or trauma locks into the body, it immediately begins to create a disruptive memory, a cellular disturbance, a blocking of energy, which can then lead, over time, to disease and illness, *which can be physical, mental or emotional:*

In other words, the Body remembers!

I also believe that in addition to this the body actually becomes disturbed in its natural function to heal and maintain itself until these underlying traumas or memories are released.

One good definition I have heard of trauma is that it is a *sustained negative emotion…*

Well!

Think about that!

This implies that we are all traumatized in some way or other by the negative memories we hold on to, from the day that we are born, perhaps from even before that…

I believe that this also applies just as much, if not more, to domesticated animals; many of the animals I treat are rescued from abusive owners.

It is not necessarily the case that *repeated* abuse creates behavioural problems;

In fact, quite often just *one* single incident can create trauma.

Trauma that will continue to affect that creature's life. But at least we, as humans, we can talk about these traumas, for the most part. In talking about them, sharing them with another, we begin their release.

(Those traumas that we can consciously remember, at any rate.)

Hypnotherapy tells us that there are those whose subconscious minds will deliberately bury or repress old traumatic memories.

For survival, this is an important mechanism, so that we can get on with our lives, but later in life these same hidden memories or traumas, sometimes called repressions; can create negative patterns, imbalances, phobias, fears and even disease.

We also know that the immune system is itself profoundly affected by negative emotions, notably depression, and it can take many months for function to be properly restored, until which time the body is susceptible to illness and disease.

These are all proven facts,
Pointing to one obvious overall fact-
The body is affected by negative emotion/trauma.

So, when an animal is traumatized or in pain, one finds it in a state of defensiveness,
Manifesting behaviour which is protective, fearful.
This may also show up physically as tight, splinted, muscle, which, in turn, irritates underlying nerves, and may lead, over time, to stiffness, joint problems, even lameness....
Horses will try to run away from fear and pain, this is natural to them.
They cannot tell us what is bothering them in any other way.

I see *Trauma* manifesting as:
1. *Physical problems*, which would include muscle tension and stiffness, lameness and tiredness.
2. *Emotional/behavioural problems*, beginning with fear and leading to a lack of trust and the inability to cooperate.

3. *Mental problems*, such as skittishness, anxiety and a lack of confidence.

These will all be covered in various degrees in this book, by example.

Obviously, I make no specific attempts to diagnose or treat horses,

Actual illness and the diagnosis of conditions is the domain of the medically trained veterinary.

Let me be really clear on this: *I am not a diagnostician, nor am I a medical practitioner.*

In some ways this book is about people as much as it is about horses.

What applies to one may well apply to another,

Yet horses are to be respected as a separate species with unique needs,

Unique awareness,

For me it's about proceeding with kindness and patience,

Never attempting too much,

Never forcing the release of pain and trauma,

Always respecting the personal space of that suffering being.

I might spend only a few minutes with a horse the first time round,
Just allowing it to get to know me,
Allowing it to feel *safe*…

Without the feeling of safety, it is difficult, if not impossible to help.
Conversely, feeling safe will encourage a horse to share these buried traumas, these painful memories.
To release the pain holding it back from a full and joyful life.

Trust is another way of engaging the process of healing.
The ensuing pages will demonstrate, through many examples,
How these two essential things:
Safety and *Trust* are applied.

Here is a first example:
This is my third visit in two weeks.
Krumpet is a three-year-old mare, retired from racing because she was not good enough; was not winning any races. She has been rescued.

Today she seems friendly toward me, receptive, distinctly more awake than the previous two sessions. She has already filled out, looking less gaunt, less like a clotheshorse.

I now stand to her left side, my hands raised slightly away from her body.

I begin to tune in:

Suddenly I 'see' several men in bright yellow 'Day-Glo' jackets, jostling about.

There is a sense of fear, confusion, and panic coming from Krumpet.

The pressure of men hemming her in: there is metal, metal bars at her sides, no escape from the pressure and pain....

I tell *Cheryl* and *June*, who are standing by, and are the rescuers of *Krumpet*.

They immediately confirm that this is the kind of clothing worn by racing stewards, or starters...those responsible for getting the horses into the starting gates.

Could they have caused the deep traumas to her left flank?

Could the heavy metal stall gates have pressed in on a very nervous mare to force her in to the starting gates?

I do know that the previous week, my second visit to *Krumpet*, I had picked up, *Tuned into* three separate injuries or traumas:
The upper neck, just below the poles.
The mid-thoracic area, moving over to an area on the left ribcage just below this,
The left lower lumbar area and left hip/femur head.
These traumas had revealed themselves in an immediate and clear way: this horse had been injured in three places, possibly at different times, but all on the left side.

The week before that, on my first visit, I had met with a wary mare, clearly not at all trusting of men, and therefore *'numbed up'*, cut off from the pain of her earlier racing life, her life in the fast lane.
So I did what I always do when I find a horse this traumatised- as little as possible!
My approach with this first session is to just make the initial contact, to show that I offer care and love, not pain and trauma.

The horse remembers this, and the next session brings with it the memory of the first, and becomes more effective through it.

I find that patience and cooperation are first principles in treating a traumatised animal.

So it is now three sessions on, and Krumpet is showing herself to be a mare with a sweet and willing nature, which has all this time been hidden under layers of tightly protective and armoured muscle.

She settles down as `I move my hands, now to the area around her upper neck, then to the midback and ribs, and finally to the left lumbar and flank.

All the while I have not touched her, my hands are about a foot away, and she has relaxed completely, her head drooping down, eyes closed…

Now at last she trusts me and her healing has truly begun.

Coupled with such loving care and support from *June* and *Cheryl*, her recovery is now not only a possibility, but a certainty.

It is always a pleasure to work with such people, those who love animals and who make every attempt to understand them, to know what is going on inside their tortured souls.

Also in the care of *Cheryl* and *June* is a mare called *Erika*.

My sense with *Erika* is one of a massive covering up over her heart, though not, of course, in the physical sense.

This is meant metaphorically, in the emotional sense. One could sense the pain there, the lack of trust, the fear of being betrayed..

She had closed down, in an attempt to protect herself from further pain and hurt.

Erika had been rearing up, bucking.

I sensed that this had been to create a temporary dampening of the pain in her lower spine.

Placing my hands over that area gave me a feeling of heat, of inflamed tissue, deep in the body.

Also there was the sense of irritated underlying nerves, which had probably led to the long-term problems she had been having in her legs…

She had suffered repeated abscesses and lameness,

Was this also a subconscious attempt to keep her from being worked?

44

Very possibly, it is something I come across all the time.

The words *'soul retrieval'* seem very apt in dealing with horses like *Erika* and *Krumpet*.
Both mares are inherently willing; one senses a sweetness in them, in spite of their abuse they are not angry, they have had to protect themselves by shutting off, going within themselves.

This is an aspect of my work I have found hard to describe in words.
It seems to me to be a kind of shamanic process, an entry into another dimension with the soul of that animal, to a place where a healing can happen, silently and invisibly. *Something, at the level of the soul, which has become lost in the soul world, can be retrieved, brought back to this world.*

I am only the facilitator of that healing, a witness. In fact, *witnessing* would be a more accurate way of describing this particular area. Often I have been this witness, this silent observer. I share in the memory of that trauma, that abuse, that misunderstanding, that inappropriate schooling. More accurately, the horse decides to share *the memory of* that trauma with me: I share, I witness….the actual healing comes from beyond that, but it is the way to it, the pathway. Some might call it compassion, this witnessing, this sharing. It is done without judgement, and without ego.

It is quiet, it is kind.

It is open, it is gentle.

It is loving,

It leads back to Unity,

'One-sciousness'

Chapter Five: *Attitude.*

I try to take a little time, by way of preparation, before
a session with a horse, To calm and neutralize myself,
Keeping my own thoughts, worries and concerns out
of the way,
Focussing on the present moment,
Being *Present.*
Being there in *Stillness,*
Being *Still.*

Some people describe this process as *'getting out of
your own way'* and I like this idea, I feel that it's an
accurate description of the attitude required…
That way, the information received whilst working
with a horse is not ambivalent, not muddled by my
own inner noise, my own subjective judgments.
*This could be compared with getting clear reception
on a radio, free from interference.*

It's also important to remember that horses are
affected by your moods:

Fear, anger, sadness and other negative feelings are felt, tasted and seen by animals-

Dogs will often respond to your anger by barking at you, horses by trying to take flight....

Ever noticed that?

So, the second thing, after stillness, is:

No Fear.

If you think about it a little, fear is our greatest enemy.

It stands between us and everything significant in our lives.

It can hold us back from going forward courageously into something new, it can prevent us from allowing change into our lives.

As someone once said: *'without change, butterflies could not exist'*

On the other hand, fear is close to respect, a healthy respect for the power of nature: the elements, the weather, the tidal changes of the sea, the hazards of fire and flood.

The hooves of a restless horse!

These are healthy fears, more like cares.

The fear I have called the enemy has more to do with a sustained negative attitude toward life, which can become a bit of a bad habit.

The fears we imagine are always bigger than the actual events.

Really, what we fear most is embracing our own magnificence, the bigger reality of who we really are and what we are capable of achieving!

In that sense, fear is a *reduction mechanism*, which affects our consciousness and awareness. It narrows us down, *reduces us, it makes us less.*

It creates separateness, divides us from each other, Separates us from that state I have called ***One-sciousness***.

What unifies us, what brings us together is ***love***.

I do not mean this in the sense of sentimentality, what some people call *'touchy feely'*. I mean love in the dynamics of its ability to unify, the activity of which brings us back to wholeness, that which *heals*.

Another useful attitude is that of:

No Expectation.

In this respect it is therefore not useful to have too much information,

I find, too much data about the animals before I begin a session.

Afterwards, of course, it can help to corroborate or fill in the details.

In other words, I feel it is best to start with a clean slate, with no preconception, no prejudice from another person, however well meant.

People will quite naturally want to bombard me with facts, with as much information about the horse as they can muster. This will sometimes become incredibly detailed.

I ask them, politely of course, to hold back on all of that till after the session, until after I have *'tuned into', listened to* what's going on.

This is not always easy for them!

Although it might sound callous when placed out of context, it is important, I find; as part of an attitude of mind in the healing process, not to care about results…

I will cover this in more detail in another chapter, but it is worth repeating here, as it is an effective way of getting ego out of the way,

Along with those methods already mentioned.

Don't get me wrong: there is nothing wrong with wanting to see an animal get well, *but expecting results,*

Being attached to results,

Is tied to ego and the ego's constant need for

approval….

Expectation can get in the way of a Healing.

Finally, an attitude of friendliness,

Goodwill,

And even *Good Humour* is helpful.

Do you know that horses have a sense of humour?

Oh yes, they do!

I have good laughs with many a horse; they love

friendly fun as much as you and I.

It goes without saying that animals have something of

personality about them, as I'm sure any owner knows,

and obviously I can't help liking some horse more

than others,

I think it actually helps to *like* a horse you are treating,

To have an attitude of *Goodwill*, a friendly openness,

Openness to becoming a friend,

(Short of actually falling into favouritism.)

I certainly have had my favourites.

Once a horse is treated it will not forget me,

In fact, I find that when I return for a follow-up visit,

That horse will immediately relax even before I start the work.
It is a satisfying experience seeing just how willing these creatures are, to be healed.

There is no belief-system to get in the way as there is with humans, no resistance on the part of the horse;
It simply offers its co-operation, its willingness to be better, to become Whole.
If only we, as humans, could be this willing and open to be healed,
Free of the restrictions imposed by our belief systems.
These restrictions include fear, conditioned response, and judgement.
It's quite involuntary, isn't it?
The way our minds assess things, constantly, judging this and that, it is habitual, and in prevents us from seeing things the way they really are.
Judgement, the way we think about things, gets in the way of Intuition.
If we want to evaluate with the eye of Intuition, we have to make strenuous efforts to suspend intellectual judgement, without, however, losing our sense for observing what comes through our senses; inwardly and outwardly.

In this way, there is so much we can learn from our brothers and sisters in the horse-kingdom.

They observe, *without judgement.*

They assess, *without preconception.*

They love, *without conditions.*

They accept, *without bargaining.*

Of course, you might say that these things are difficult, if not impossible to achieve, for us humans.

Certainly they are not easy, but neither are they impossible.

It's simply a matter of creating positive habits, breaking the old ones

So to recap, in the context of creating the appropriate conditions for a *Healing*

to take place, I have found the following attitudes to be useful.

1. *Be still, be present, and get out of your own way!*
2. *Have no fear.*
3. *Have no expectations (of results)*
4. *Have an attitude of goodwill, humour or friendliness.*

This is not to say that having this approach will automatically bring about the *Healing*. Far from it – good intentions on their own are not enough. However, I have found it useful to adopt the above attitudes as a positive habit of soul, which then becomes conducive to *intuitive healing.*

Chapter Six: *Horses have wings...(I allow myself a little poetic indulgence)*

At first I kept it to myself, mainly to avoid ridicule,
And secondly, because I wanted to be sure,
To *really* understand what I was seeing.

And it was and it is this, simply this:
Just there, at the withers, the root of the neck,
Horses have wings...

Starting out, without a thought,
I found my hands just going there;
It felt so right, I just did it.

I *felt*, then *saw*, then *knew*,
That the wings are the *key*,
The door to it all for me.

Today I can sense that flow, feel that energy:
It is the health of the horse, its life and its strength,
It is something I just *know*....
In the wings,

There is colour, shape and size,
There is *Energy*, the state of things.
In the wings,
There is *Information*, *Content*,
Memory and *Event*.

So I go with this information:
Here, at the place of the wings, is a special place, a
place where energy flows in and flows out. I can feel
it in my hands; sometimes I can see it inwardly,
As colours, shapes, forms, and a sense of wellness or
lack of it.

I find that when a horse lacks energy, these *wings* will
droop, lose colour and vibrancy, and go grey. When
that horse is healthy and happy, however, its wings
will stretch to support it, be strong, and show colour
and vitality.

Pegasus, the winged horse, is now no longer a myth
for me,
This is real! I can feel and see those wings!
They are the *life-energy* of the horse,
Made manifest!

Then, to cap it all, to confirm my thoughts, my brother
sent to me, from America, from the Metropolitan
Museum of Art in New York,
A reproduction of an ancient Chinese golden horse.
Right there, on the withers, at the root of the neck,
There are wings, shown as flames..........

These days I find that those *wings* to be very
individual, much like faces are to us. As part of the
Healing process, I visualize them as being strong,
carrying that horse, giving it flight, lightness and
agility.
And I find that horse immediately begin to respond, to
become light and powerful, to become, once more
what it always was, a horse, whole and complete......

On the other hand,
When I first place my hand there, at the onset, I feel
Whether the *'energy'* of that horse is flowing, as it
should....
This will include the emotional state, the mental state
and the physical state.

The first time I began to work with this awareness, I was surrounded by a group of interested riders, all with horses in that particular yard.

Most of them in that circle felt changes within their own energies whilst I was working on the horse, though these ladies were several feet away.

Some even said that they felt spaced out or tired afterwards, others that they felt energised...

Some did not take kindly to the *experience,* some were even a little afraid.

An important point, at this juncture, would be to repeat that I am merely a *conduit for Healing to take place*.

I am, I believe, a *facilitator*.

A crude, but effective analogy would be *that I am the jump-leads, not the battery that starts the engine*.

Energy flows through me, within that horse the energy then responds,

Aligns itself,

Corrects itself according to ancient and immutable laws of creation,

Restores **Wholeness**, **Love**..

These laws are beyond my conscious understanding…

I can't explain *how* it works; only that it *does*!

Chapter Seven: *Grief.*

Occasionally I will find a horse, one that is held in grief, unable to *'move on'* emotionally, and therefore not able to *really function at full potential.*

Grief manifests emotionally in human beings in various ways.

Elizabeth Kubler-Ross, author of the best seller: *'On Death and Dying'* offers the formula *DABDA,* which stands for:

Denial,

Anger,

Bargaining,

Depression, and finally,

Acceptance.

This formula applies both to those who are dying as well as to those close to that person; their partners, family and friends.

It does not necessarily follow in that particular order, but it certainly applies.

I have come across horses and dogs affected in this way.

Norma was such a case.

One very depressed mare.

I was asked to see her, as she was listless and not eating with her usual enthusiasm.

I stepped into her stable and gently laid hands on her:

Imagine my surprise when I saw this 'other horse' standing right beside her, but not in the physical sense.

A dappled grey mare, taller than Norma, with a black mane.....

With this image was a powerful feeling of sadness, it welled up within me at the same instant.

I asked the owner, whom I will call *Cara*, if *Norma* had a *'special friend'*.

She had:

A mare matching my description.

But this *'special friend'*, said *Cara*, had died 18 months previously, following several protracted illnesses, beginning with loss of her sight.

She had lived in the neighbouring stable, right alongside *Norma*!

Cara responded to this information by bursting into floods of tears, and in so doing, released, I believe, some of *Norma's* grief.

She was amazed, as people always are when they encounter the emotions of animals, even feeling a little guilty that she had not recognized the symptoms of *Norma's* sufferings.

Not surprisingly, *Norma* responded positively, immediately after this release.

Her mood lifted,

She was free....

The following week when I visited the yard, she was sprightly, eating well, and taking an interest in the goings-on in the yard around her.

Her depression had gone.

Sometimes I come across a mare suffering depression as a result of being separated too early from her newly born foal.

Perhaps this is another form of grieving.

Worst cases are those of stillborn foals and it is heartbreaking to see.

Some owners leave the dead foal with the mare for a time,

Usually, so far as I am told, for twenty-four hours.

One client told me that she left a dead foal with the
mare for three days.
After this time, she was still inconsolable, and the
body had to be removed.
So her companion of the fields, another brood mare,
was brought into her stable.

It worked; they dealt with her grief together.
Horses are social animals,
They help each other in astounding ways,
Often taking on the foal when the mare dies,
Working as a caring community within the herd.

I feel it is important to know that sharing a pain is the
beginning of it's healing.
Just by recognizing the suffering of another sentient
being we begin to help to bring about it's healing.

I will devote the next chapter to what I call *'Cellular*
Memory', which is a description of this process of
locking in trauma or negative emotion.

Seeing or recognizing this trauma begins to effect the release of pain, or even in some cases, heals immediately

Chapter Eight: *Cellular Memory and Listening*

One of the first direct experiences that I have had of
how the body holds onto traumatic memory,
intuitively speaking; was with a dog.
There have been many subsequent cases, with horses,
cats and humans, some of which will be accounted for
at length in this book.

So I shall tell you of a spaniel called *Rory*, who first
put me in mind of what I have come to call *'Cellular
Memory'.*
I was called out to see *Rory*, as his owner was
concerned over the way he was barking incessantly,
when left on his own.

As I put my hands on the dog,
I was immediately given a *picture* of him being
dragged down a flight of stairs by an irate and
impatient owner.
The details were pin-sharp.

Rory had been fitted with a choke collar, which was at this moment very effectively choking him. It was made of a chrome chain.

I saw a man dragging him forcefully down the stairs. The man was clearly out of his depth with the animal, not connecting with him. He was seeing the dog as a huge inconvenience, leaving him alone at home all day.

Strangely, the fact that he was gay seemed to be important information. Why?

I was soon to find out.

As I fed this information to *Rory's* new owner, the response was immediate and powerfully affirmative:

'Yes!' she said, this was all true.

She went on to confirm that the animal rescue centre had described *Rory's* former keeper as a *'very angry gay man'*, who had no time for the dog, and yes, he had used a *choke-collar*, which had left marks of chafing on the poor animal.

Rory's behaviour changed for the better, immediately after this first session.

He stopped the incessant barking when left on his own and lost his former aggression.

Of course he was glad to see his new owner when she returned home, but now he was calm and content in his new home, no longer anticipating being dragged around on the end of a painful chain. I saw *Rory* on two further occasions, each time he showed more improvement and was decidedly more relaxed and at peace with himself and the world.

Here is another case involving cellular memory, this time in a horse that I shall call *Mary*.

Mary was suffering with severe back-pain and behavioural problems;

She had progressively become skittish and unpredictable, shying away from innocuous things and making a simple ride out really dangerous for her owner....

I visited *Mary* at her stable-yard and gently made myself known to her, taking my time before going into the box with her.

On placing my hands on her,
I was immediately presented with a picture of Mary
falling over onto what looked like a huge pile of
concrete and builder's rubble.

*I also saw a man in a dark green jacket, behaving
quite brutally toward her.
Here also was his green RangeRover standing by,
along with a sense of exactly when, the actual time it
all occurred.*

These details were all confirmed as being *Mary's*
previous owner.
She was struck by the details of his vehicle, a green
Range Rover….something I would have no way of
knowing, as he lived several hundred miles away.
Mary showed an improvement from that very day,
losing all fear and calming down.

This example, and the many others that followed,
whether they are dogs, cats or horses, made me think
this:

*Perhaps it is enough to recognize the sufferings of
another Sentient Being to release its pain….*
Sharing a burden by talking it over with a counsellor
seems to do people a great deal of good, often
effecting a complete *Healing*, and certainly beginning
the process.

But what if you are a being who cannot talk?

What then?

How can you release your pain?

How can you heal?

And who will listen to you..?

This is then how I think *'Listening'* works, in the intuitive sense.

And *Cellular Memory* may be one way in which all sentient beings can communicate with us, however negatively that may be.

This is why, as I have mentioned before, I have called my craft *'Horse Listening'*. Because that is what it is.

People ask, *'How do you do this'*, or *'what are you doing'*

The accurate answer, so far as I know, is that I am *'listening'*.

Listening requires *stillness*, being quiet in the mind.

Stillness is a prerequisite, I believe, for *Intuitive* work of any kind.

This can be difficult for me, especially as the owners, quite rightly, want to communicate with you, want to tell you what has happened, and when.

They want to tell you that their horse is not

Performing.

Being *Naughty.*

Not *Behaving.*

Not *Level.*

Pulling on the left Rein.

Pulling on the right Rein,

Refusing to take the Jump,

Not *Happy,*

Not *Eating Properly*........etc.etc.

And sometimes, very tactfully, of course, I have to
suggest that they talk to me or question me at the end
of the session, rather than during the course of it, as I
prefer silence, in order to *'listen'* more effectively.
So *Intuitive* work also requires tact
You can't tell people to shut up!
Well, not if you want to be asked back, anyway!
Equally, I sometimes need time to ponder
information, rather than blurt it straight out,
immediately after a session. It might take time to
absorb, to understand the information just received, to
unscramble it, to translate it into words that will make
sense to someone else.

There is no point in alarming people or frightening them with things they may not understand or even cope with…..especially when sometimes you are having trouble understanding it yourself, or where further reflection is needed.

I know that I am still learning to be this person called a *'Horse Listener'*
But I am at least certain of two things,
I love doing whatever this is that I am doing, seeing these beautiful beings respond,
And I want to continue to be a part of that…
Making whole what is not.

Chapter Nine: *Carrying the Burden*

This is probably one of the most important things I have to impart to those who keep and ride horses. Probably the same thing applies to ALL domestic animals….

It is a difficult thing to explain, harder even to accept, and it is this:

Animals can feel OUR pain!

Yes, this is so!

In fact, they not only feel it, but they take it on, *they carry it!*

I am sure you have noticed how, when you are in a bad mood, or feeling off-centre, that your horse reacts, perhaps becoming aggressive, uncooperative, less than willing?

Dogs and cats will *'read'* you, knowing immediately what's going on with you.

Some say they can smell you.

(We certainly have it in our language…the *smell* of fear…)

There is a word for this carrying of the emotions of others, feeling another's pain, and it is: *'Empathic'*, they feel *empathy* for our sufferings.

I have a friend who says that cats are like sponges for stress.

She says that they will come over and actually sit or lie on you to absorb your negative energies.

If this is so it could make us view domesticated animals in a different light altogether.

What if, in addition to this, they can sense what we are *thinking* and *feeling*?

Sensitive owners/riders will know exactly what I am saying here.

Many feel such a strong bond with their horses, or cats and dogs, that they tell me that the animal will sense when they are about to go away on a journey, or a vacation, or move stable-yards, long before it happens.

Similarly, they also sense our every mood, and knowing this can help you build a stronger connection and trust with your horse.

However, this is not a *'how-to'* book, and I make no claims on how to train horses!

This is a book about experiences.

Here is one that may illustrate the notion of *empathy*.

Julia called me one day, asking if I dealt with
behavioural problems in horses.
Yes and no, I said, in my usually direct way, let me
see if I can help out…
Julia met me at the yard.
Straight off I could tell that she was very agitated.
Her energy was that of an angry person, accentuated
by her flaming red hair!
She took me over to the stable to meet *Sharp*, who
was pacing about furiously, with the same kind of
energy as *Julia*; this was not a happy horse!
I suggested that we move the gelding into the yard
outside, where I could keep out of range of his angry
hooves.
It took four grooms to persuade *Sharp* to leave his
box.
Definitely, I find it is never very sensible to share a
stable with an angry, unknown horse!
Not first time round, anyway.
So *Sharp* was tethered outside, to the side of a barn.
He didn't seem any happier there, but I wasn't taking
any chances.

Julia told me that he was very *'fresh'*; that he had been trained as a racehorse, that he enjoyed speed, but lately had been badly behaved, unpredictable and difficult with the grooms;
All except one, *Laura*, who seemed to have a way with him, so I asked her to stand with *Sharp* while I tried to lay my hands on him.

As gently as I could, I stroked *Sharp*, speaking soothingly and keeping where he could see me, but where I could be out of reach of his hooves.
All I wanted from this session was to connect with him, to create a trust between us.
A horse will always remember you, and *I wanted him to remember me as someone he could trust.*
So after around 15 minutes of skipping around some very threatening hooves, and managing to put my hands on *Sharp* for about 2 of those minutes,
I called an end to the session and made an appointment to see him the following week:

Something was very wrong.
I could not get through.
I couldn't connect with this horse.
Was I losing my touch?

What stood between us?

I pondered on this.

Laura had a way with him.

So why didn't I?

Perhaps he had a problem around men, many horses have, often as a result of harsh experiences with them, usually the *'breaking-in'*.

I would have to wait and see.

The following week I saw *Sharp* again.

This session was *slightly* easier.

He allowed me to spend time with him, but still the restlessness, the defensive crooking of rear legs, in preparation for *you-know-what…*

Afterwards I took *Julia* to one side, and to my own amazement and hers I asked her if she had been through some emotional upheavals in the recent past.

Acting on a hunch, I felt I just had to ask…

She immediately clammed up and abruptly said that she had to go, and that she would see me the following Friday, same time.

She then turned and strode off, obviously angry.

Something had *touched a nerve*;

I knew that from her response.

I don't ever pry into people's lives, preferring the way in which things reveal themselves, in their own good time.

So questioning *Julia* in this direct way was not my style, hence my own amazement when I found myself asking her!

But it had worked in some way.

I was soon to find out how.

The next morning the phone rang.

It was *Julia*.

'Sorry about the other day, you were right to ask me. I should have told you…

She then told me the whole sad and shocking truth.

She had been abducted during an armed robbery some six months earlier, and was held hostage for three days.

It was in all the national newspapers.

Although *Julia* had not been *physically* harmed, she had suffered severe emotional trauma; she had been unable to sleep for weeks, still suffered from recurring nightmares and was not able to go back to work.

She had been to a counsellor a few times, and that had helped.

However, being alone with men made her very uncomfortable and she did not know if she would ever get over this….

Poor girl, my heart ached for her.

Naturally it was far easier for her to talk to me at a distance, over the telephone, and now, of course, *Sharp's behaviour made total sense*:

Like her, he could not endure the company of men.

Like her, he was angry and listless.

Like her, he was unable to relax and enjoy life……

I returned to the yard the following Friday, as scheduled, to find that the trusted groom, *Laura*, was not there.

Neither was *Julia*, who had sent apologies and some cash…

I was left to get on with it, along with a groom I had not seen at the yard before.

So I did. I just got on with it!

And do you know? It went really well.

Sharp was calm, even *friendly*.

All four hooves stayed firmly on the ground and he looked, as a moved my hands over him, as if he was really enjoying it, relaxed and happy.

I did not see *Julia* again after that, but she phoned two weeks later to say that *Sharp* was back to his old sparky self, but free of the anger and resentment: she could not believe the change in him.

He was enjoying life and all the grooms felt the difference.

Now they were all happy about going into the stable with him, and his appetite had picked up.

As for her, she was considering further therapy, but was getting through things, and had a new job.

There are many horses like *Sharp*.

Many owners like *Julia*.

I come across them all the time.

Certainly I do not wish to make owners feel guilty with the statements I made at the beginning of this chapter. I only wish to invite them to become responsible for their thoughts and feelings,

To become aware of how our *thoughts and feelings* affect our environment.

Negative thoughts and feelings can be seen as negative energies.

My wife Debra, who is a psychotherapist and knows about these things, says:

'Thought is living energy…'

After all, if you think about it, everything is *energy*, is
it not?
All things in the physical world are basically made up
of the same stuff,
The difference between you and a plant or you and an
animal or a stone has to do with the way in which this
stuff is *organized*,
And the kind of *intelligence* that has organized it, that
lives within it.
But really, the essential components, the building
blocks are the same,

There is a *connectedness* between all things,
The *self-conscious awareness* of this living energy,
As well as how it all connects within us,
This is what makes us human.

Chapter Ten: *The Homestead.*

Gypsy was probably the biggest horse I had ever seen.
This was early in my career and I was still very green,
still learning.
More than a little nervous, I approached this gigantic
grey mare.
She immediately turned her back on me and retreated
to the back of her stable, showing me a pair of huge
defiant buttocks!

Heather, owner of *Gypsy* and *The Homestead* tried
her best to reassure me:
*'She does this to everyone, don't worry…she'll let you
know if she's going to kick'*
Cold comfort.
I was terrified.
I could see myself being dropkicked over the yard,
sailing over the roof, two mighty horseshoe
impressions on my nether regions…
What was I doing here?
*Where did I get the idea that I could help giant horses
with attitude?*

Somehow I gathered myself and gingerly advanced.
As I laid my trembling hands on *Gypsy*, her response,
predictably enough (considering my lack of
confidence), was to retreat; in fact, she barged past
me, doing another circuit of the stable, as if I wasn't
there at all.

What was I going to do?
Again, I advanced, putting my hands gently but firmly
on her withers and lower back simultaneously, feeling
for her *'wings'*, but keeping well away from those
ample hind hooves…

To my surprise she relaxed immediately I put my
hands on her,
Letting me into her space ~
For a full ten minutes, *Gypsy* settled down, lowering
her immense head, lips drooping.
Eyes closed.
In that short interval I located, intuitively, old trauma
in her right shoulder, deep down inside the tissues. I
resisted the impulse to palpate those tight muscles:
instead, I simply placed my hands there and waited.

Suddenly she started up out of her reverie, as if remembering this irritating human in her space, and once again I was barged into the sidewall of the stable.

My first audience with *Gypsy* was over.

Nonetheless, I had made that all-important first contact, however brief, and she seemed to enjoy it.
Some of it, anyway!

The next week I was back.
This time things went better and I was able to spend more time with her.
I was barged less and together we were becoming cooperatives in her healing.

An excited *Heather* greeted me at the yard gate, as I arrived the following week for the third session with *Gypsy*.
She told me that a couple of days after the second session with *Gypsy*, a large swelling had appeared over the right shoulder, at the *exact place* I had laid my hand.
It was not, I discovered, tender to the touch.
It was soft, apparently filled with fluid.

This fluid was reabsorbed into the body within a couple of days.

Gypsy seemed more alert, *Heather* said, less grumpy, better in herself.

This mare had always been a bit bad tempered, and the grooms learned to keep well away from those giant hooves.

Heather was keen to tell me something else she had forgotten to mention to me before: that some time before my first visit to *Gypsy*, her vet had discovered, after x-raying the mare's shoulder, that there were structural problems deep within the shoulder joint, too deep to get to.

This was the same shoulder that had manifested the swelling after my visit.

Heather told me that *Gypsy* recognized the sound of my arriving car, and would be waiting there for me at her door…(enter *Gypsy, the gentle giant*!)

I saw her intermittently at *The Homestead* over a period of years.

Sadly, she is no longer with us, but is far from forgotten.

The Homestead was always a place I enjoyed visiting, several other horses were stabled there, and I visited one or two, including *Bea*, a chestnut mare, whose arthritis appeared to respond positively to my ministrations.

I can remember cold winter mornings warmed by toast and tea, in the small kitchen attached to that stableyard.

Sharing breakfast with us were several chickens, who were afforded equal status with the feeding humans and were allowed to pick crumbs from the table or wherever they found them.

In fact, I administered to one of these chickens, a speckled hen called *Peggy*, so named because of the absence of a foot, lost to a marauding fox.

Peggy paid me with her own eggs, an arrangement which suited us both well, until sadly, a fox took her away entirely.

There was always something interesting going on at *The Homestead*, usually a rescued animal of some sort, including, for a while, a marmoset monkey...

The people who worked there were linked by their love of animals, and it was a safe haven to many a passing creature.

Chapter Eleven: *Tonic*

Horses are by no means my only clients.

I also see many dogs, though perhaps far fewer than horses.

I shall be devoting time to them later on, in a further volume.

I have also treated several cats, and I am going to tell you about *Tonic*, the ginger tomcat, who has since left this world, but his story deserves being told....

I met *Tonic* whilst visiting my brother in *Carbondale,* in the *Rocky Mountains USA*, over a wonderfully white Christmas some seven or eight years ago.

His very worried lady-owner asked me to take a look at him, she said that he was unable to eat or drink comfortably.

It was something to do with his neck, she said, could I come as soon as possible?

So I went to see him. I had only a few more days in the country.

Now, the thing about cats, I find, is that they seldom need anything at all! In fact, they seem to allow us the great privilege of feeding and caring for them, even though they will often remind us that they don't really need us, *know what I mean....?*

In all humility I will admit that I had never treated a cat until then.

Tonic duly padded into the lounge and after circling around me a couple of times, checking me out, he flopped down in front of me and submitted to my hands.

Well, amazingly, as I *'connected'* with poor *Tonic*, I immediately *'saw'* him being attacked by a man wielding what looked to me like a large shovel.

The scene was very clear:

The man was wearing a bright red sleeveless puffer-jacket.

'We' were in a narrow back-alley, it was cold and snow lay thick on the ground; on all sides there were high buildings and metal escape-stairs, it was just like a set from West Side Story.

Somehow I knew that this was New York.

The man I was seeing was hitting Tonic with what I now know to be a snow-shovel, and the worst blow

had caught him in the neck…somehow the cat had
escaped the attack, badly wounded as he was.

When I told his lady-owner what I was *'seeing'*, she
became very upset at first, realizing that she had been
powerless to save her beloved cat from this attack, but
confirmed that she had moved to the *Rocky Mountains*
from *New York* with *Tonic* only weeks before my visit
to them.
She knew nothing of the incident I was seeing, yet she
did confirm that this was exactly the kind of back-
yard neighbourhood in New York City that she and
Tonic had lived in for a time.

Immediately after this transfer of *information*,
Tonic got up off the floor and left the room.
I knew he would be back.
She said, *'Shall I fetch him back?'* and I said
(knowing the way cats like to stay in charge), *'no,*
don't worry, he'll be back…'
And, sure enough, less than 5 minutes later *Tonic* the
ginger tom came back, making directly for me, where
he flopped down at my feet!
You know the way cats do when they have decided to
relax….

This time I literally went straight for the jugular, working firmly but gently on the tight traumatized muscles in his neck.

I could feel how incredibly *'splinted'* the whole area was, the tight armouring of muscles effectively preventing the poor animal from moving the neck or in fact, swallowing food and drink with ease.

Obviously, at the moment of impact from that snow shovel, the body had taken defensive action, and the muscles in the neck and shoulder were still in that mode of deep protectiveness!

After tolerating my ministrations for a couple of minutes, *Tonic* got up again, this time going over to his food bowl where he started eating enthusiastically! He paused only for a moment to look over at me, meeting my eyes, and blinking, as if to say, *'Thanks dude! That sure feels better!'*

We were all touched at this moment and knew that a *Healing* had occurred.

I had an email from *Tonic's* lady owner just a few weeks ago, telling me that he had died a little while ago from old-age, but that he had gotten so well after that session, and was calmer and more content in himself…

Tonic for all of us.

Chapter Twelve: *Sensitivities, Allergic Reactions and Parasites.*

Something just wasn't adding up here.

Dallas, a chocolate mare, was streaming from nose and eyes.

I had now visited her several times and she had released a lot of tension from her back, she was now less stiff and more cooperative, said *Kara* her owner, but *Dallas* was just not happy in the yard, preferring the fields to her box.

The vet had been called in.

He had done a lot of tests: blood tests had eliminated the obvious, she did not have anything viral or inflammatory, yet here she was, still clearly distressed and producing masses of mucous, streaming from eyes and nose…..

Kara was herself an extremely sensitive soul, one whom one might call *'empathic'*, picking up all the negative energies from others.

She did not get on with other riders at the yard, and when I was called in,

I got the clear impression of scepticism, if not standoffishness from them!

They did not seem sympathetic toward the problem, seeing me as a crank called in as some kind of neurotic response to an incurable problem.

Those kinds of things have never really worried me, since I am well aware of the unusual nature of my work, and the defensive response it can meet with.

I cannot take responsibility for the reactions of others to my work.

The antidote to it is the joy of seeing finally, at the end of the day, a happy and healed horse!

This is what changes attitudes of doubt and scepticism.

So here I was, emptying my mind and trying through *stillness* to understand *Dallas's* problem.

'Show me how I can help this horse', I asked Spirit *simply*.

Suddenly, without warning, I began to stream from nose and eyes.

This was so uncomfortable; I wanted to run out of there straight away….

I resisted the impulse and did not.

Instead, I bent over and picked up some of the bedding off the floor.

There was an immediate sharp chemical smell, which burned at my mucous membranes. *I was being shown!*

Was this the problem? Was this a chemical intolerance to the bedding?

I had a very defensive response to this idea from the others in the stable-yard, which, incidentally, was one of those very large roofed barns, subdivided into many boxes for the horses.

This was a working farm, with tractors coming and going, cows lowing next door and lots of activity all round.

A typical British farmyard.

Everyone in this stable-yard used the same bedding for their horses, but it seemed that only Dallas had this (possible) reaction to it.

At this point I was assuming that the offending chemicals were in the wood-shavings used as bedding, so I went over to where it was stored in a neighbouring barn.

There were stacks of the shavings, piled up in polyurethane bags.

One of these was open, and there was that same toxic smell, reminiscent of pesticides and chemical treatments....

At that moment the farmer's wife appeared at my elbow.

She had one of those ruddy round faces, tempered by the outdoors, and she was cheerful and forceful all at the same time.

I expected trouble, after all, what business had I poking about in her barn?

A stranger in the yard, doing even stranger work...!

Amazingly, though, when I told her that I thought the bedding smelt of chemicals, she dipped a large red fist into the bag, put the shavings to her nose and....

'Whew! What a stink' she assented, she who was used to the funk of pigs, cows, chickens and their waste products, not to mention related malodorous stuff in the day-to-day life of the farm.

So here was an unexpected ally, someone else who could confirm the toxicity of the bedding.

We changed *Dallas's* bedding to simple untreated straw and the streaming of nose and eyes stopped.
Why the other horses did not react to the shavings I do not know.
I can only offer the following explanation:
Stress is accumulative, this we know to be so.
Whether it is mechanical, emotional, mental or chemical, stress may sometimes only manifest once the body has tried over a period of time to disperse it, finally without success.
Then the accumulated stress appears as illness, as disease, as allergic reactions, as muscle tension.
The fact that *Kara, Dallas's* owner was so sensitive and empathic herself is significant, at least to me.

Did they attract each other, being alike in this way, or was *Dallas* carrying and trying to process her owner's stress?
I cannot answer with any finality, but changing the bedding solved the problem.

Moving now to the subject of parasites, worms in particular.

Again, it is not my place to utter medical prognostications, or in fact to offer opinions on treatments, that is the work of the veterinarian. However, sometimes things happen which seem to cross over that space between us, if in fact there is one!

I was called out one day to see a grey pony called *Sabi*.

His owner was one of those very busy people, who seem to dash about constantly; this was to become a theme in the treatment of her pony.

'How soon can you put him right?'

'How many treatments will he need?'

Fair enough, but I had not seen him or laid hands on him, we were now just walking towards the stable-yard.

My first impression was that *Sabi* was an extremely agitated and aggressive little pony.

He stood there glowering, angry and uncomfortable on the end of a rope.

His entire body was tense, hard with tight muscle, and he was perspiring and seemingly set to go off like a rocket given half a chance!

Clearly this was a pony in some distress.

I turned to talk to his owner, but she had moved off already, there she was cleaning something with a hose….

So I gently put my hands on *Sabi*, who tried to shy away.

This was not going to be easy!

He was not having any of this!

What came to me intuitively, as I felt the stiffness in his body, was that this was something to do with his brain.

His eyes popped and stared, his legs shook, there was something, literally turning inside his poor head…

He did calm down though, within a few minutes of my laying hands on him, but the stiffness remained.

I agreed to see *Sabi* the following week, briefly chatting to *Jo*, his owner.

She again wanted to know how quickly I could fix him, and then something prompted me to suggest a course of *Aloe Vera* juice.

I had read an impressive article written by a vet, on the efficacy of this ancient remedy on the treatment of parasites, worms particularly.

I can only remember that the article proved, with scientific validation, that it worked, there were complicated proofs, to do with blood and blood platelets.

Anyway, it is a popular, and I might add, harmless plant, useful for burns, wounds, and even taken internally as a pick-me-up.

Many owners say they can see immediate effects after the ten-day course, coats become shiny, appetites improve, they say....

I also remembered seeing a horse afflicted with red-worm, it had spread to the brain.

Symptoms included shaky legs and skittishness.

Of course, I did not want to alarm Jo by suggesting that Sabi was red-worm infected, *and it is not my place to deliver a diagnosis, as I am not medically trained.* But I did ask her if he had been wormed recently, and she insisted that he had been.

However, she took the advice and put him on the *Aloe Vera* course, as I said it might help to calm him down, and it would improve his overall condition.

The following week he seemed much better, he was not grinding his teeth, and allowed me to work on him without shying away.

He was also not perspiring and was not quite so bug-eyed.

But the stiffness remained, and his legs still shook.

Jo had decided to have his head scanned, she said, she was concerned that it might be coming from his brain: perhaps it was a tumour or something of that kind, she said…remember, I had not said a word about the brain, so she went ahead and did this, and no tumour was found.

The vet, however, suggested that the symptoms *could* indicate red-worm infestation in the brain, so the pony was duly going to be blood-tested the week after.

In the meantime, the *Aloe Vera* course was at an end and *Sabi* had endured three sessions from me.

Then, suddenly, everything changed.

Jo phoned to say that *Sabi* had relaxed, was keen to work with her, and appeared to be happier in himself.

She was going away for a few days, so could I see him in a couple of weeks?

A fortnight later, when I arrived at the yard, there were smiles and welcomes, even the offer of a cup of tea, which is always welcome…!
Jo said that the blood tests were negative, but that the scan had shown *some evidence of red-worm in the past.*
Sabi, however, was now healthy and worm-free.
In addition, I could feel that he was relaxed and free of shakes, altogether a happier little pony!

This was an unusual case.
It had no precedent, and there has been none like it since.
Whether it was the *Aloe Vera* that had evinced this rapid recovery, or whether it was a combination of the imbibing of this harmless plant with my ministrations , I cannot say.
What is important is that the pony got well.
Very well.
I saw him once more a week later, and he all was well in his world, although I would have loved to suggest to *Jo* that she slow down a bit…just a bit!

Chapter Thirteen: *Healers and Vets*.

This is a difficult one.

I believe that most vets consider *healers* to be a little flaky.

Perhaps it is partly because we do not come from a rigorously scientific background and are not trained in a recognized institution that we are not generally respected, or even accepted by them.

Partly also because it is difficult, or even impossible, within the current materialistically based scientific parameters for us, *as healers*, to prove that what we do has observable/provable results.

How do you prove that a horse *has regained its soul, or that it has released a deep emotional trauma from the past?*

How do you validate that it had that particular problem to begin with?

Difficult.

My position on this is that I will always require clients to make their vet aware that their horse or dog is undergoing *healing* from me, *and that the vet approves of this.*

There is also a legal implication in this, and I see my work as complementary to that of the professional.

I have never actually clashed with a vet, in terms of the work I do.

In fact, quite to the contrary:

I have found that, especially where there is a kind of diagnostic impasse, where the vet has not been able to get to the bottom of a problem, or where the animal has simply failed to respond to conventional treatments, I have always been welcomed into the *'circle of healing'*.

Vets are, in any case, kind and caring people; doing, like any of us, the best they can in any given situation. It takes a special person to work with animals in the dedicated way in which they do and I have only ever had admiration and respect for them.

They, on the other hand, would be willing to admit that they are on unfamiliar territory when it comes to *intuitive healing*, and dealing with *emotional trauma*.

There is, I believe (based on my own experiences), more and more cooperative work being done between conventional and complementary modes of healing. Particularly as complementary treatments or *healings* can act preventatively, taking the pressure off already-overworked vets.

In other words, a potential problem can be dealt with before it actually manifests physically. I will try to explain this a little more clearly:

I met a *'Medical-Intuitive'* whilst on a healing course in America some years ago. In fact, I went to a talk she was giving on her particular healing craft.

She said that she had started out as a nurse in an Accident and Emergency unit in a busy hospital in New York.

She was able to *'see'* into the bodies of accident victims as they arrived, providing accurate medical assessments to the initially sceptical interns.

After a while, she said, the interns began to respect the accuracy of the *information* she was receiving and more, they came to totally rely on the data she was giving.

Why not?

After all, lives often depend on split-second decisions based on *information*....

This gifted lady went on to become one of America's most respected *Medical-Intuitives*.

Furthermore, she is also able to *heal* her clients once she has seen their problem. She says that her gift allows her to see, within the *subtle energy body* or *aura* surrounding the physical body, indications of disturbance.

In fact, she says it is possible to find there that which would only manifest physically a month or two further on….

In other words, *she can act preventatively, at the level of the etheric or causal body to prevent disease from actually manifesting!*

Most of the cases she deals with are those for whom there is no apparent cure, many are terminally ill, only to be *healed* by powers working through this remarkable lady.

I have, in my own way, treated a number of *'write-offs'*, where the vet has endorsed my intervention, and in some cases they will actively refer me.

Twice now I have had vets, whom I have never met, actually refer animals to me as a last resort.

On the first occasion, I was referred to see a dog called *Harry.*

The vet, whom I had not met, had heard of me
through a client, and since he could do no more for
the dog, he said, why not try me?
Nothing else to lose…

This very lazy, but amiable black *Labrador* is a
rescued dog, suffering from early arthritis.
The vet's prognosis was that he was incurable and
should be put down, as he would only suffer more as
time went on.
I had been seeing *Harry* regularly for several years; he
just recently died.
His loving owners, for indeed they were, knew when
he needed me, and he was always so relaxed and
sleepy that it was an effort to hold him up for long
enough to effect the *healings*….

Chapter Fourteen: *About Attachment to Success and Failure*: *Lessons Learned.*

'There are no horse problems, there are only people problems'…Anon.

Years ago, whilst still studying to become a BSR practitioner, I was taught to see success as a dirty word.

Or put more accurately, *to not make success my prime motivation*, rather, to put everything I could into each session, doing my absolute best,

Then stepping away from whatever the result might be,

It's really about not being attached to that result, whether *successful or not*.

This was a change from the normal view, from seeing failure as a dirty word.

Here are a few examples of cases I would not describe as successful, yet each of them has, sometimes painfully, taught me something, or led me to some important discovery; and therefore helped to make me more effective as a *Healer*.

As I ran my hands down *Boris's* spine, I could immediately tell that this was a horse with some serious back problems.

I had been called out to this busy yard in the depths of the *Surrey* countryside to see him, referred to his owner by a friend whose horses I had been treating.

Boris had been trained very specifically for the purpose of hunting, now outlawed, but then very active and popular.

Also, there were at least two other riders who shared the use of him.

This always makes things a bit more complicated, as riding styles differ from rider to rider, as do weights and attitude….

Anyway, enough excuses, on with the story:

His owner wanted to know from me initially, over the phone, how many sessions it would take *'to put the horse right'*, *it was the hunting season, and he wanted to hunt!*

He had to!

I said I didn't know how sessions the horse would need, that I would have to see *Boris* first, but that *three to four sessions* were the kind of minimum for a horse with back problems.

Little did I know how *literally* my words would be taken!
I have since learned not to make any kind of commitment without actually *seeing the animal first.*
Obviously

First Lesson *learned*: *Don't commit to anything without seeing first!*

So here I was in *Boris's* yard in deepest *Surrey*, being closely watched by a man whose only aim was to get this piece of horseflesh back under him, so that he could enjoy himself in the hunt again….
(That was, I honestly believe to be the attitude of the man, nothing personal.)
My first impression was that this was a horse in need of a vacation. He was stiff and sores everywhere. His lacklustre coat shouted out his poor overall condition. He felt out of sorts and unhappy in himself, just exhausted really.

Boris twitched and shied with every move I made, he was clearly in some pain, just looking at him made me uncomfortable.

In addition to all this, he was sway-backed, more than a bit underweight, and definitely poor, as far as the musculature was concerned.

This indicated, for me, deep tensions underlying the surface.

I found it very hard to focus, as if the expectation of success itself was holding the healing back....

I did what I could with this first session and made an appointment to see the poor creature a week later, somehow avoiding the kind of detailed assessment that was expected from his owner, only advising rest from any kind of strenuous work.

I was relieved to find, on my second visit to *Boris*, that his owner could not make it and I was left alone with him, a groom stood by to hold his head-collar, but she kept a respectful distance.

My second impression of *Boris* agreed with the first one: everything about this horse shouted: *'I am exhausted!'*

However, he had improved from the previous week, and this was something confirmed by the groom, who also reported that *Boris* was still being worked, which was contrary to my earlier advice.

So I called his owner, this busy London professional, and left a message for him to call me back.

When he called back, he said that he was *'concerned that he could see no visible improvement in Boris.' This was the second visit I had made, and the horse still held back. Nothing had changed,* he said.

He was *disappointed.*

Three or four sessions, I had said, *would 'sort him out'*, he reminded me

Two had made no difference.

When I suggested that *Boris* be rested entirely for a couple of weeks, it was as if I had suggested something totally irrational....like having him fitted with wheels, or launching him to the moon!

'Rest?' he shouted down the phone, *'Impossible!' 'We have all these events booked up and paid for. I cannot possibly rest him....'*

I began to feel a bit ridiculous, as one does, when under this kind of pressure.

Maybe *I* was being unreasonable,

I lacked confidence as it was, reminding myself that I had only been at this work now for a little over two years.

So I compromised, against my better instincts, and went for the option of working him in the sand school for a week, but without saddle or rider, even though that didn't feel quite right either.

Second Lesson learned: *'Be firm and listen to your instincts!'*

When I revisited the yard, he still didn't seem much better, so this time I put my foot down; after all, what did I have to lose? I insisted that, despite his commitments to those forthcoming events, he should give *Boris* a complete rest for at least the next two weeks, possibly longer...

These last two words were not well received, but he agreed to think about it and call me back. As it was, he was away on business for a week, so he would give me (*Boris*, rather) that week, no more.

I was thinking only of this exhausted horse, he really *did* need a break, and that was the information I was getting…

The third visit found a much-improved *Boris*. He looked more relaxed, there was less evidence of stiffness and tension. His coat looked better.
The groom reported that he seemed more sprightly, was eating with a better appetite, and was good on the lunge.
I set a date for the following week, reminding them that he still needed more rest.

My final visit to *Boris*, the week after, was a terrible shock.
His owner was there, pacing about, clearly ruffled.
He reminded me of my *'commitment'* to the three to four sessions.
This was the fourth and Boris was just as lame.
I asked whether he had been ridden, and without meeting my eyes he confirmed that the horse *had* been out on the hunt, just a day after the last time I had seen him.

We could not wait any longer, he insisted, and *things should have worked by now*, he said pointedly, *if they were going to work at all!*

No, he was *not prepared to allow any more of this*, and that was that.
A month and four visits later, he said, and *what did we have…?*
A lame horse…

So that was it. I felt crushed, I was taking it personally.
I had failed.

Third Lesson *learned: 'Don't take things personally!'*

I had no further news of *Boris* after that, I only hope he came to no harm.
Poor old *Boris*. Poor old me. I had done my best to make him comfortable.

Fourth Lesson *learned: 'Always do your best, you can't do more than that!'*

In quite another context, I one day found myself,
unexpectedly, with an audience of five ladies.
Word had got out that this *'horse person'* was going
to be treating an ancient mare, which had been
deemed, somehow, untreatable by the local vet.
I have to say, the poor animal was as thin as a stick,
every bone staring out from stretched skin.
It did not look at all well, and stood very unsteadily
on its matchstick legs.

I proceeded, under ten watchful eyes, to run my hands
over this poor veteran, finding very little in the way of
supportive muscle around the spine and hindquarters.
It was not, according to the owner, rideable, and I was
not surprised, on inspection, to find that she had said
so.
After a while I made an error of judgement and
decided to loosen the mare's tight shoulders by giving
them a gentle stretch. This I did by carefully
stretching out each foreleg in turn.
(After all, I had an audience to impress!)
Bad idea:

With little or no support from the wasted muscles in
her back end, the mare was not able to lean away from

the shoulders as I stretched them, which is what would normally happen.

What I would *expect* to happen.

Instead, five pairs of eyes watched me *as the mare, in slow motion, toppled forward onto me as I bent in front of her to stretch her forelegs…!*

There was no way I was going to lose face in front of my audience by ending up on the ground with a skinny mare on top of me!

Somehow, I still don't know how, I managed to push her upright again, saving her and me from a disgraceful fall.

***Fifth Lesson** learned: Don't show off!*

Of course, there were and there still are other lessons to learn, other *'failures'* to recognize simply as being lesser degrees of success.

Every one of them can only serve to hone my skills as a healer, becoming opportunities to improve my approach to helping and healing horses.

I look back on these lessons I have learned with gratitude, thanking each and every person(and animal) for bringing me closer to being more effective.

And, of course, I can have a good laugh at
myself..now!

Chapter Fifteen: *More Meetings with Vets.*

Lebanna, a chestnut mare, had been suffering from a condition known as *'kissing spines'*, a crude term to describe what is seen as the deterioration of the discs between vertebrae, resulting in a literal contact or *'kissing'* between bone and bone, on the anterior aspect of the spinous.

Not a pleasant condition, one which is usually seen as incurable.

Nina, the mare's owner, asked if I could meet with her and the vet at the stables, so that we could have a chat about *Lebanna*.

There the vet, an amiable Australian, explained to me what this condition meant, how it was not curable in the conventional sense.

He did seem genuinely interested in my approach, and so I explained as best I could what I do, what I was about to do:

I told him that I could not do the horse any harm, but that my approach would probably take time to effect a *healing*, in response to those tight, protective muscles in the spine, which were, as I saw it, causing the problem.

I could not help feeling that he was humouring me, he didn't stop smiling as I spoke.

He then went on to describe *his* way of dealing with the condition, and that was to take a chainsaw and simply cut away the spinouses on top of the vertebrae, effectively causing them to fuse together…*end of problem!*

For a moment I thought he was pulling my leg, but he wasn't.

I felt quite ill, thinking about his description of the procedure, and almost begged him, at that point, to allow me to try my gentler approach before he resorted to applying this drastic technique.

There was another problem with *Lebanna*: She suffered very painfully when in season, which, in turn, brought on severe attacks of colic.

I suspected that this was a strongly contributing factor to the stress and tension in her whole body.

So, with the approval of her vet, I began treating her. To her credit, *Nina*, her owner, hated the *'chainsaw healing '* idea as much as I did, so she agreed to some long-term treatment from me, which went on for around six weeks.

There was a definite improvement to begin with, and we saw her becoming much more relaxed within the first three weeks....

At that point her hormones took over, and she was, at this time, not able to do more than stay listlessly in her box. She was obviously in some pain, and unable to work.

I felt this was something I could not help her with, I felt so powerless, it was awful seeing her like that.

Then she suffered a huge colic attack and the vet was called in.

I treated this ailing mare twice more, and then I had no further contact with her or *Nina*.

I would like to think, though, that my work made a difference to *Lebanna's* life.

I certainly did not hear of her having to go through the *'chainsaw procedure. '*

Then there is *Twizzle*, probably one of the most challenging clients I have had.

His owner called me to ask if I could come out and see him.

This horse had been, quite literally, collapsing under the rider!

The vet had been called in; she thought the horse might have back problems,

And she wanted to be there when I came over to see *Twizzle*.

So I agreed to meet them all at the yard.

As I ran my hands down *Twizzle's* spine, I could feel knots of tense muscle, armouring or protecting the spine.

He winced and pulled away as I touched these areas. My work as a BSR practitioner has given me a lot of experience with spinal muscles, and I could already tell that this was a horse with trapped and irritated spinal nerves, this as a result of prolonged muscle compression in the area.

Everything about him shouted this out.

What can happen, with prolonged spasmed or compressed muscle bearing down on the nerves, especially on the sciatic nerve group, is an immediate and dramatic loss of strength in the legs, resulting in sudden collapse.

I have seen this occur in human beings, and it is distressing enough, but try to imagine this occurring in a horse with a rider on it's back.

This is what was happening with Twizzle:

Sudden collapse, with the rider and horse falling to the ground

When I heard this, I felt that trapped nerves were the obvious deduction.

Also, I noticed that there were very distinct areas where muscles had become *'poor'*, where there was wasting of muscle due to underlying tension…

The very young vet watched me intently while I worked, asking now and again what I was finding. She was newly qualified, and had a wonderfully enthusiastic approach to her work, concerned first and foremost for the suffering and well-being of the horse. She also seemed to be very open-minded about my being there…..

So I told her, and *Twizzle's* owner, that I felt confident that the problem was in his spine, and that he really ought to be rested up for a good while to help recovery; to allow for the release of these spasmed muscles.

I recommended at least six weeks rest, which raised eyebrows with his owner,

but the vet nodded her assent. She agreed strongly that the poor horse needed rest more than anything else, and that riding was not an option.

I suggested regular visits from myself over that period, once again insisting that this was a structural problem, and that because of that I could not guarantee a complete recovery.

As far as I could see, this was a serious case, and one could only hope that *Twizzle* would respond; that with enough rest and healing treatments, the tight, armoured muscles would gradually relax, and release the underlying trapped nerves.

Another, relatively minor concern from the owner was the presence of two lumps, which she thought to be sarcoids, along the edge of the spine.

These would not be helping the poor horse in terms of riding comfort either.

So, with the blessing of the young vet, I began my regular visits to that yard.

I used a combination of different techniques in this instance: *Firstly, BSR to stimulate the release of muscles. Next, energy or natural healing on the energy system, with the 'wings' as the focus; and finally, light pressure to certain acupressure/meridian release points.*

My suggestion was that *Twizzle* should not be worked *at all* initially, then, as an interim measure, worked in the sand-school with no saddle or rider on him for a while, and then we would see how things went after that.

Hopefully, we could gradually introduce more exercise as and when we saw some recovery.

Fortunately the owner and the vet agreed to all of these suggestions.

At first there seemed to be no improvement.

In fact, he seemed to get worse.

His owner was a little alarmed over how stiff he seemed after that first session with me, and of how grumpy he had become....

I reassured her, citing many cases such as this, where things appeared to get worse before they got better. I told her that this was typical of spinal problems; or more specifically, of spinal problems caused by muscle tension.

Trauma to underlying soft tissue and nerves would only gradually release, and this release could be painful and uncomfortable.

'No feeling, no healing', I quipped; quoting a phrase we often use in the application of the BSR technique. This really describes the process of previously trapped nerves gradually signalling the release of overlying muscle by *'coming back to life'*

One had to be patient and trust the process, I said, convincing myself also in saying this: after all, I had no idea of whether it would all finally work.

The weeks went by.

With the third and fourth weeks, *Twizzle* had progressed to being gently worked in the sand-school. His attitude had changed for the better.

He was enjoying the work, and the grumpiness had gone.

Also, I could now palpate, or apply mild pressure to the affected areas of the spine without any reaction from the horse. For me, this was a sure sign of progress, a sign that the muscles were relaxing as intended.

After two more weeks it was possible to put a saddle onto him and gently ride him in the school.

He was now strong and confident, and I set an appointment for a couple of weeks ahead, cautioning against going too fast and too hard with him....

Well, here's how it went:

A month later his owner phoned me, very excited, very pleased indeed!

Twizzle had just won his dressage event, she crowed,

Not only that, but the sarcoids on his back had completely disappeared!

She could not believe it.

It was a miracle, she insisted.

'Thank you, thank you, thank you!' she said,

Smiling down the telephone!

I too was elated, thankful myself, once again seeing *Spirit* at work in the process of *Healing*.

The trust, patience and care invested in this suffering horse had paid off.

Chapter Sixteen: *Clearing Negative Energies in Places ....I digress a little.*

Inevitably, as an *Intuitive Healer*, you sometimes come up against some challenging energies, which we are wont to call *negative*.

What does this really mean?

Some say that what we perceive as *dark* or *negative* is only an opportunity in disguise, meaning that once that particular challenge is met, there is growth, progress, even release...

Another way to understand this is that when we are in a state of fear, our energy is vibrating at a lower frequency, which then, in turn, attracts *negative energy to us* (not unlike a magnet), which includes *negative emotions,* such as fear, anger, resentment and depression.

(I have covered this process elsewhere in the book, in describing the attitude of mind, which I require of myself as a prerequisite to *healing*.)

Conversely, when we are in a positive state of mind, when we are in a joyful, happy or peaceful and centred state, our energy is vibrating at a higher frequency, which then attracts *positive energies* or *emotions*.

These would include love, joy, happiness, and an attitude of goodwill.

It's easy to understand then, what a responsibility we all have towards those around us, through the energies or emotions we project outwards.

This will explain why, when we feel down or depressed, anxious or fearful, we seem to attract even more of the same negative stuff!

'What a day I'm having' = *more of the same stuff.*

The Law of Attraction suggests that what we are feeling inside ourselves, whether it's

positive or negative, good or bad, attracts more of the *same* to us

So:change the energy in yourself positively, release the negative thoughts and feelings about yourself and others, and the world around you will respond, for the better.

I have been to places where it does not feel at all comfortable, where it is hard work to effect a *Healing*, just because energies in that place are low, negative vibrations.

One such place where I have visited horses, and which I cannot name (it is a working yard), is a prime example.

It is known to be haunted by a dark past.

During the 17th century Catholic priests were tortured and hanged there, and believe me, the horses sense this and are not comfortable there
It is as if the dark cellular memories of that time are still there, I could sense them, where they were at their strongest, in the area adjacent to the sand school, which is also where the horses would shy away….

Of course, there are psychics and clairvoyants who can accurately *'read'* this information, often with incredible detail, citing names, dates and events
Some of them are capable of exorcising these darker energies, which I am told are usually departed spirits, people who have died violently or suddenly and who have been prevented from *'moving on'* into the realms of Light because they are stuck in that lower energy, of *fear* or *hatred*.

They are simply afraid of letting go and moving on into the Light. They can be stuck in a time warp, sometimes, I am told, for a long, long time.

Sometimes they are people who have died so suddenly that they do not *know that they are dead*, in a place without a physical body.

There are many books on this subject, and I only mention this as it affects animals also, who are highly sensitive to these entities, as well as to our own darker energies whilst we are alive.

Quite recently I read of a case, where a horse would always become fearful and rear up at the same spot, in a field.

The rider called in a professional clairvoyant who was able to tune in to the energies there.

What she found was the soul of a departed airman from the Second World War, wrapped in his parachute, having died before he could leap from his stricken plane. *This is what the horse was seeing, no wonder it was afraid.*

What was interesting was that when questioned about that spot, *the farmer confirmed that* he *had found the wreckage of the crashed fighter plane at the exact*

place in the field where the horse had consistently
shied and reared up with fear.

The Clairvoyant went to that place, was able to
communicate with the soul of that dead airman,
explaining to him that he had died, and that it was
now his time to *'move on'* to the next place, to the
Light.

I am told that he did, and the proof of it was that *the*
horse had no more fear of that place.

I digress…I have described this case specifically
because sometimes such things will occur. Animals
are far more sensitive to these energies than people,
and there is clearly a need for some understanding to
be brought to it.

I have found other, less dramatic instances where
horses have been unhappy about their living quarters
due to negative energies in their environment, and in
each case there has been a profoundly positive
response to a move.

The Chinese art of *Feng Shui* has much to say on
these things, and provides practical advice on what
can be done to balance energies in the home and

surrounds, it is interesting to note how even running water under a room can have severely negative effects on *'chi'* or life-force, and therefore on the occupants of that room.

Clearly, this applies to animals too. Recently I advised the successful relocation of a restless horse to a different stable, simply because it was responding negatively to an *electrical distribution board* in it's stable.

The first year I began my work as a *Horse Listener*, I found myself in a place where the entire house and the people in it was affected by negative energy.
I noticed that the ponies I treated there were listless and often aggressive, and when I went into the house, I felt very ill at ease. Something was not right.
Whilst treating a pony, the owner's little girl hung about, and as I looked up and smiled at her, she stuck her tongue out at me!
Her rude behaviour then, and on several subsequent occasions, quite shocked me. Then, in that same place I treated one of the dogs, which was having seizures. Something was going on here. I became convinced

that this poor animal was picking up the dark energies
around him, perhaps even trying to process them.
Eventually I decided to mention this to the owner.

I told her that I felt the place needing some
energy/space clearing, and in fact,
I offered to do this myself, with a couple of friends
who are *healers*. She agreed to this, so I came back
with my friends, to do some *'ghostbusting'*.
We covered the entire house and every room in it,
We cleared the yard, the stables, the garden and the
outbuildings.
There was a distinct feeling that a dark presence,
which had been overshadowing the place, was now
lifting and departing.

After the *'clearing'*, I could feel a new calmness in
the place, as well as with the animals.
Strangely, however, the owner said it all felt *'empty'*.
Significantly, that entire family, mother, daughter,
father and son all undertook to have therapy shortly
after, and it became pretty clear to me that the
negative energy was in some way, connected to their
own issues.

There were many unresolved conflicts within the family,
Acting outwardly like a negative force field,
Affecting things randomly around them, especially those animals.

Was there not also, perhaps, something already there, on that farm, which acted on the family as a psychological trigger, bringing out their issues? Or was it the other way round, as previously suggested?
I don't know.
What I do know, however, is that Healing began right there and then, and that it continues………

Chapter Seventeen: *Feeling it in the Body: Clairsentience*

There are those I know, who, as *Healers*, feel *in their own bodies* the sufferings of others.

This ability is called *Clairsentience*, literally meaning *'clear feeling'*.

It is a rare and useful gift.

This gift gives those who have it a very direct, and for them, irrefutable, means of monitoring pains and diseases in the bodies of their clients, *by quite literally feeling these issues in their own bodies.*

Up until now this has not been the way for me, it is not my particular gift, but there have been some amazing exceptions.

Here then are some of them:

I am standing in the stable of a tired-looking horse called Magic.

This is the second or third visit to this particular yard. I have already treated several horses there, all with different problems.

*Amongst them is Norma, the grieving mare I have
mentioned in the first chapter of this book.
So now a group of curious women, riders and grooms,
stand crowding at the stable door, leaning in to
watch.
There is an air of expectation.
I am being tested.
I am being referred to as 'The Horse Whisperer' and
my visits are generating some excited whispers on
their part, not all of it welcome on my part!
I see the title 'Horse Whisperer' as an inaccurate
description of my work and a distraction to what is
really going on. There is honestly no sort of glamour,
as I see it, around my work, and no need to stand in
awe of it.*

*I have become an experiment. The ladies of the yard
have conspired together to present to me a horse
whose problem they all know about. The horse,
perhaps aptly, is called Magic. This tired bay is
showing as much interest in me, his new visitor, as an
empty feedbag!
Well...maybe a bit more than that, but here I am,
being observed.*

Several ladies crowd into the space in and around the stable door.

There is an air of conspiracy; they all know something I do not.

Even so, it is all in the spirit of fun, and no one is really sceptical, since they have already seen some results from previous visits.

Then it happens:

Suddenly, as I lay hands on Magic,
I feel my heart begin to race,
Uncomfortably fast, and irregularly;
Now I know I have a good heart, no physical problems there,
And I have not been drinking coffee.

So, knowing it is coming from Magic, I blurt out, without hesitation:
'Does this horse have a heart-problem?'
'Yes', is the immediately affirmative reply.
'He does!'
There is a moment of stunned silence and then a lot of surprised looks and chatter amongst the ladies crowded at the door.
I have passed the test.

In fact, as it turned out, just days before,

Magic had been medicated by his vet for this heart

condition, and was known to have a heart-murmur.....

Then, not understanding that this would prove taxing

to him, his rider had evented Magic the following day,

in spite of the strong medication he was on.

Though he seemed willing enough, this had clearly

strained his heart,

Exhausting him.

And this is what I was feeling when I put my hands on

him :

His pain in my body.

You will remember another time something similar

occurred, when, through Dallas,

I experienced the streaming eyes and nose as a result

of chemical reactions.

It is not unusual for me to experience strong

emotional empathies with horses,

Especially when they are feeling heart pain, grief,

depression.

At other times, a horse will protect itself from being

overwhelmed with pain.

Then, it will close down the *heart centre*, figuratively of course.

When this happens, certain signs can identify such cases:

Dullness in the eye,
A listlessness or lack of enthusiasm,
A lack of interest in the world around them,
A diminished appetite.

Are these not the same signs we see in human beings who have *'shut down'?*
Numbed themselves to their hearts in order to survive?
You will remember Erika, the mare I mentioned at the beginning of the book.
She had done precisely this: *shut down her heart in order to survive.*
Obviously, I don't mean her *physical* heart, what is meant here is spiritual; the heart as an organ with emotional responses.

Coming back to the faculty of *Clairsentience,* though.

Dallas and Magic, amongst others, have shown me yet another *intuitive* way to monitor what is going on with them, *by feeling it in my own body*.

Whereas the faculty of *Clairvoyance, the ability to see that which is hidden from normal sight*, is more available, more accessible to me, it has not precluded the occasional glimpse into other modes, other spiritual senses.

These could be seen as tools, *gifts given to us by God,* in order to allow us to be of service to others, to help others more effectively.

Certainly it is my view, and others would include *animals*, not just humans.

After all, are we not all of us God's creatures?

Chapter Eighteen: *About problems between horses and men....Respect*

This is a difficult issue, and bringing it up will not endear me to some readers, but I feel I must once again speak out on behalf of the horses.

It is the issue of men. More specifically, the issue of the rough treatment meted out to horses by men.

There are problems with many horses I have treated that go back to the way in which they have been backed, handled and trained.

And so there are some who are permanently shy of men, due to earlier traumas suffered at their hands.

Of course, this does not preclude women, but by far the highest incidence of horse abuse is by men, in my experience.

Usually it is to do with the brutal, forceful domination by men in the training process;

So what we find then, typically, is the horse that will shy away at the presence or even the sight of a man, by association.

What's to be done then?

For that I have no specific answer, other than to hope for more enlightened times to come, and to continue in my own small way to help to put things right.

My work is to help the horses that have suffered in this way.

One such horse, one of many that I treated for this problem was *Max*.

Max was a coal-black horse, backed in Ireland, who would habitually run to the back of his stable any time a man came by.

He was clearly very frightened, rolling his eyes and even breaking out in a sweat.

So I went to see *Max*.

With difficulty, I managed to touch him gently, soothing him with quiet words,

I did not force myself on him, taking care to respect his space.

He really did try, poor *Max*, to cooperate. I suspect it was more out of fear of what I might do to him if he didn't, than willingness.

I spent only a few minutes with him, just to make the first tenuous contact, then left.

The following sessions, over a period of seven weeks, were a gradual process; developing trust and clearing trauma from the past.

Max started associating my visits with pleasure, rather than the pain he linked with men.
I worked at his pace, never forcing, always honouring his feelings.
If he shied away, I let him be.
If he came to me, I rewarded him with hugs and kind words. (Not carrots or sweets)

Sound familiar? This is elementary psychology, isn't it!
But here's the thing: it *works*! (I believe that horses and humans are, mentally, much closer than we think. Horses are certainly able to think logically, just as we do, and from this, they have developed the ability to choose, just as we have.)
From here it's a short step to understanding that it's possible for a horse to want to choose the soft option, the option that involves *lest pain and force*.
I'm getting ahead of myself here! So on with the story and back to *Max*:

On the fifth session I arrived at the yard to find *the miracle had occurred....*
Max trotted up to the stable-door to greet me!
He nuzzled me with his soft, relaxed mouth, meeting my eyes without fear.
He was cured!

I returned two weeks later just to make sure.
His owner said that her husband was amazed to find just how affectionate *Max* had become.
In fact, he was quite taken aback. This was not the horse he used to seeing the back of.
It was the same with any other male visitor.
With the healing application of patience, love and kindness, together with my regular ministrations, *Max* had got over his fear.
Forever.

Max is only one of many horses needing help for the abusive treatments meted out in their tender, early lives.
It is an epidemic.
So sad,
So avoidable,
Yet so curable.

Perhaps men feel threatened by the size of horses, by their intelligence.

Their power and strength, held in check by dignity and kindness....

I don't know.

There are alternative backing and training techniques available, which are not brutal and terrifying to the young horse.

Amongst those, (and I have made passing reference to it before), the *'Join up'* technique of *Monty Roberts* stands out.

I have seen it demonstrated and can testify to its effectiveness.

There is *no brutality or violence, no attempt to dominate through fear*.

There is trust, gentle understanding, allowing the horse to work at its own pace.

Monty Roberts calls the body language of the horse *'Equus'*.

He spent time with mustangs in the wild, watching horses communicate with each other, watching how they used their bodies to speak to each other.

He noticed that obstreperous behaviour of young colts caused them to be pushed out of the group by the dominant mare, there to face predators without the protection of the herd.

They were ostracized by all until asked back into the circle…..

Out of this, along with many other observations, came the method of *'Join up'*.

I mention this system particularly, only because of its being based on the *actual social behaviour of the horse*, rather than the needs of human beings….

It is a system based on *trust*, where the horse more or less trains itself.

It respects the intelligence of the horse, allowing it to choose to cooperate.

It is a system that both understands the body language of the horse and actively works with it. We can learn from this wonderful symbiosis of horse and trainer, certainly the proof is in seeing it actual work.

Certainly there are other techniques, equally effective, equally respectful of the horse.

One of them is the *Native American* approach, where bit, rein and bridle are nowhere in sight.

Instead, a relationship is established, a mental rapport between rider and horse.

When the rider has a mental image of where he wants to go, what he wants to do;

The horse senses it, sees it, responds to it.

It's a matter of focus, of concentration.

It's a partnership, cooperation between rider and horse.

Chapter Nineteen: *Terminal Cases*: *Time to Let Go…*

Sometimes I have had to treat a horse where it has become apparent that nothing can be done to save it. Knowing this, and acting on it, requires tact and sensitivity.

It's about saying goodbye, often to what is *an old friend*, a *friend who might be really tired and is now ready to move on…*.

One such case was *Herby*.

Herby was one of group of horses, which still includes *Tuppence*, *Flight* and *Spice*, whom I treat on a regular monthly basis.

These horses are retired, having all led a busy life eventing, show jumping and winning prizes.

Now, at the end of their working lives, they are lovingly cared for, and this is where I play my regular part; providing maintenance treatment every four weeks at *St.Ives Farm*, near *Hartfield, East Sussex*. This is one of my favourite places to visit.

Sue and Peter run a tearoom at *St. Ives Farm* during the summer season, and one of the perks of my visits there is an occasional cream tea to refresh me after my work!

St.Ives is a busy place, there are peacocks everywhere, owls, horses, dogs, goats and sheep....I just love going there!

The place hums with life, *animal life* especially.

You can have your tea, watch the farm bustle around you, and be buzzed by low-flying peacocks and sparrows artfully begging crumbs from your plate.....

Below you the valley opens out for miles around into the sweetest vista of green hills and forests, the quintessential Sussex countryside.It is a stone's throw from Pooh Corner, childhood haunt of A.A.Milne.

(No, this is not an advertisement; *St.Ives Farm* is not sponsoring me!)

So, now to *Herby*.

I arrived at the farm one day to find *Herby* with a very swollen tongue and mouth.

Sue thought that a wasp had stung him.

When I treated him, he was jittery and obviously uncomfortable and in pain.

I got the feeling that he just wanted to be left in peace, so I did what I could to *stream some healing energy through him*, and then left, having made an appointment with Sue to see him soon, the week after.

With the next visit the mouth and tongue were as bad as ever.
Still swollen, and now there was a large swelling on the lower-jaw as well.
He had stopped eating.
I tried to gently *heal* the area, not actually touching him, holding my hands about six inches away from his mouth, but he immediately responded by shying away and walked to the opposite side of the stable.
He did not want to be helped, certainly not by me, perhaps not by anyone.
Not on that day.

I spoke to *Sue*; she had a resigned look about her when I spoke to her.
She knew.
A day or two after she called me to tell me that *Herby* had, mercifully, been put into his final sleep.
He was in a lot of pain, and was asking for that final release.

We miss him, but his time had come, and he had made
that clear to all of us.

There is a time to heal, to hold to things body and
soul, to return to wholeness,
Equally,
There is a time to let go,
To allow
That return,
To wholeness.

Life and Death in the physical world are equal
statements of its reality...
There is a time to let go.

When I made my visits to *St.Ives Farm*, I would
always be met by *TJ*, the friendly sheepdog. He would
escort me to the stables and, when invited to do so,
would stand by to help me. He would actually make
sure that the horse stood still and cooperated whilst I
worked on it. If it moved away or showed signs of not
cooperating, he would go for it, baring his teeth and
nipping at their feet. This alarmed me at first, then I
realized he was just doing his job!

He, like *Herby*, has moved on, and I miss his bright
intelligent eyes, the way they would meet mine, as if
to say *'Okay boss, this okay for you?'* Bless you TJ

Moving on now from *St.Ives* to another place, another
pony:
In the deep of winter I was called out to see *Oscar*.
He was one of the most puzzling cases I have ever
treated, and though you are now no longer with us, I
salute you *Oscar*, for your strength and courage.
This is your story:

In a field stood this pony, stiff and shaking.
At first glance it was clear that something was very
wrong….
He was struggling to stand upright, every muscle
tense and trembling with the effort. His owner, *Lisa*,
said that he had fallen over and had been helped up,
with great difficulty.
As I stood beside him and tried to connect with him, I
could feel his panic, shock, dis-orientation. The vet
had been called in and was perplexed.
His possible range of diagnoses suspected a brain
tumour, red-worm, epilepsy, a virus, or poisoning. He

said he could not be sure, and further blood tests were pending.

A couple of times I had to step away as *Oscar* threatened to fall over.

Lisa was very upset, she loved this pony and seeing him like this was heart-breaking.

I was getting no clear information from the pony.

As if it was all muddled up…perhaps there was more than one problem here.

Food poisoning was the first thing to investigate.

This was a field where there were a number of toxic influences.

For one thing, the owners ran a kennel for dogs, and all their waste was burned in a heap on one side of the field. Walking around the perimeter, I also came across several nasty-looking toadstools.

Lisa also told me that *Oscar* was inclined to want to munch on *bracken*, he had to be restrained from eating it. One of my clients had mentioned to me that convulsions, and possible death was known to follow consumption of the stuff. She had known of such a case and there *was* no antidote to the poison.

Then there was also the possibility that redworm had got into the brain, I have described such a case, with

Sabi, earlier in the book, but *Lisa* assured me that *Oscar* had been de-wormed regularly.

However, *Oscar* showed some improvements after a couple of sessions, and we became hopeful that he would recover. By now he was able to move around the field, although one foreleg was seemingly lame and had to be dragged around, as if there was no strength in it.

The tenacity of this pony amazed me.

He was not going to be beaten by this, whatever it was!

Weeks went by.

I saw *Oscar* intermittently.

Lisa had, by now, enlisted acupuncture and a new vet. Still the lame foreleg, though, and the stiff shoulder on the same side.

Nothing was now getting better any faster. A physiotherapist then visited him.

Her assessment was that ligaments and tendons in the shoulder and leg were torn and irreparably damaged. Whether this was the original problem or whether it arose as a result of the fall, no one can say for sure.

Lisa finally decided, after a few more weeks, that she felt that the quality of life for poor *Oscar* was not any more viable for him. He was very uncomfortable.
She was very upset to lose him.
But she had done all that could be done.
It was now time to let go.

It was hard for *Lisa*;
She had a great love for this horse.
They had spent happy years together.

Some feel that it is unfair that animals have a shorter lifespan than we do.
Perhaps it only seems that way..
I came across an alternative way of seeing this,
It has been suggested that, *if we see domestic animals as having an evolutionary cycle, which involves contact with humans;*
Where they feel our love,
Our care and cooperation as part of their spiritual evolution;
Then it seems logical for as many animals as possible to experience this contact.
Therefore it is fair, it is just for them to have a shorter lifespan.

155

*Part of my understanding of life, as it is on this
planet,*
Is that everything is part of a perfect plan;
Everything is moving just as it should,
Towards that ultimate union,
One-sciousness.

Chapter Twenty: *Toxic Places, Feng Shui in the stable.*

Sometimes I have visited horses and been informed (by them!) that they are not comfortable in their yards or stables.

Here is one such case:

A while ago I treated a wonderful eventing horse,
After dealing with his back and leg problems over a few weeks,
He was mostly better,
But still there was this *something*,
Something that was causing him unhappiness in his box....
He seemed listless, disturbed, low in energy.
What was it?
I stood quietly with him, concentrating,
Listening:

Then I heard him, he said:
'I don't want to be here, move me out of here!'
Why? I thought, in response to the horse.

Again I heard him:
'Just get me out of here!'

Then I saw it:
Running water, a stream under his stable,
This was what was bothering him,
Affecting his energy!

I told *Frances*, his owner what I had heard and seen.
She looked puzzled, but she immediately agreed to
move him to another stable.
Why not?
She was prepared to try anything, and this was easily
done.
The horse was happier immediately,
No more restless pacing from wall to wall,
No more the sapping of his energy.
He looked and felt better within an hour.

A couple of weeks later, visiting that same yard,
Frances said:
'By the way, that stream you said was under the
stable,'
'There isn't one'

She was grinning at me now, teasing me, watching me, waiting for my response, *but I was so sure…*

'*But……*' she continued, seeing my confused expression '*….there is a rainwater pipe running underneath it, though,*'

'*It feeds into the stream below the yard…*'

Remembering *Frances's* teasing, I find it interesting that *Feng Shui* exponents warn against the *negative energies created by water running under a room*, especially a bedroom.

They say it can even make people sick.

Small wonder then, that horses are affected too….

Just recently I visited a horse who remained restless and fidgety in spite of several treatments. He would just not relax in his stable. Out in the field he was fine, but not when he came into his box…

I stood with him, puzzling on it, when my eyes came to rest on an electrical distribution board on the wall of the stable.

On pure impulse, I suggested to *Cheryl* that she move the horse to another box.

Problem solved. He immediately relaxed and showed no further reaction.

159

Negative energy, this time from electrical flows.

I have had many other cases such as this one.
Horses, like most other animals, are very sensitive to
subtle energies that most people do not notice at all.

They can *sense* when someone is about to arrive, long
before we do.
They can *sense* when another horse in the yard has
died, even though it may have been *'put down'*
somewhere else.
They can *sense* when their owners are angry and out
of sorts.
Elsewhere I have described how horses are sensitive
to *'ghosts'*, to the presence of departed spirits…
More obviously, horses can find over-noisy and busy
yards stressful, to a point where their health begins to
suffer.
Recently I visited a horse that was tired and listless.
I found out, after questioning people in the yard, that
having to live in a working farmyard with tenants
coming and going at all times day and night, this
particular horse was actually suffering from lack of
sleep.

With constant noisy interruptions it was not getting a
full night's rest- young parents with restless babies
will know exactly how sleep-deprivation can make
you feel.

The problem was solved when the horse was put out
into a quiet field at night.

Horses have their needs just as we do.

They are connected to things, to Nature, in a deeper
and more profound way than we can understand.

One breeder I know, with many years of experience in
the field, (no pun intended!) insists that pregnant
mares will quite often delay the birth of a foal until
the cold and wintry east wind has dropped!

Chapter Twenty-One: *Treating Horse And Rider.*

I have often discovered the rider to be a direct cause
of back pain in a horse.

I'm talking about muscle tension in this case; where it
is clear that a horse has developed a sore back as a
result of compensating for it's rider.

I can tell from the stress patterns in the horse's back
how it is having to adapt to the eccentric pressure
coming from the riders back.

For example, where a horse is holding on to tension in
its *left* lower back, it's quite likely that it is having to
compensate for tension in the riders *right* lower back,
in other words, on the *exact opposite side*.

One look at the way in which the rider is walking will
confirm this for me.

I get great pleasure being able to help both horse and
rider, and this only confirms the degree to which the
relationship works both ways.

Sometimes I don't see this connection at first.

However, if a muscle stress pattern persists in the horse despite successive attempts to relieve it, I will check to see if the rider is making a contribution!

In cases like this the problem may be entirely physical, in which case it is a fairly easy one to remedy.

(My training as a BSR practitioner qualifies me to make recommendations at this level.)

As a matter of fact, the first thing I look for when I treat a horse is whether the problem may be arising from a physical cause, such as muscle tension.

Accidents, falls, and overuse are all physical causes potentially leading to tensions or stress in the musculature.

Where this has happened, it is a relatively simple matter to apply the BSR technique, which then stimulates healing dynamics within the horse to release those tensions.

I have mentioned elsewhere in the book the connection between horse and rider on an emotional level, and also on a mental level.

There is no level, on which a connection is not made between horse and rider,

And it is important to acknowledge this connection again and again.

Some time ago I had the opportunity to help with such a partnership. I shall call the rider *Jane* and the horse *Otto*, for reasons that will become very clear in the course of this description.

Otto was already known to me before *Jane* called me in to see him. I had, in fact got to know him quite well through visits to other horses in his yard. He had not shown any major problems until he was loaned to *Jane*. In fact, I found out later that his original owner had felt strong reservations about selling him to *Jane*, who was not content with just having him on loan. Going against her instincts, she allowed *Jane* to buy him from her.

Then the problems began. *Jane* called me to say that she felt that *Otto* was a little lame in the fore-legs (she thought); that he had been 'naughty' and she was becoming frustrated with his lack of co-operation. She had heard about me and *Otto's* owner had mentioned to her that I had seen him in the past, at his original yard.

I made an appointment to see him at her yard. My first impression was that this grey pony was not happy. He was displaying the classic body language associated with anger: *ears back, flicking of the tail, stomping of hooves.*

I did my best to calm him down, staying quietly with him, not attempting too much. *Jane* all the while, chatted on and on about what she felt was going on with him, what she had been feeding him, what time she fed and groomed him, etc etc. She also made much of her idea of introducing him to 'tea-time', where she encouraged him to join in with her in taking tea and biscuits at 4pm…At the time, it made me smile, but was later to prove crucial in the whole picture of their relationship…

With my second visit to *Otto*, things were not much different, he had not shown much improvement, still the anger, now joined by restlessness.

He was now also showing the classic symptoms of *laminitis.*

What was up?

Instinctively, I asked *Jane* if she had any back problems, and when she was puzzled at the question, `I explained that if she did have back-pain, it could be affecting the pony's spine, and this could, in turn, be creating discomfort..

She responded by confessing that she did indeed have a history of back problems, associated with her ongoing commitment to long-distance running. She agreed to see me for a few sessions of BSR, beginning the following week.

These sessions with *Jane* were very revealing. They showed up a host of issues, including traumatic emotional problems (for which she had some counselling) extending back into her early past. She was reluctant to reveal too much, insisting that she felt she had done all she was willing to do to make herself more functional. Naturally I cannot elaborate, out of respect to her (and also to do with client confidentiality), what those issues were.
It is significant though, to mention that those emotional issues were very much present, albeit repressed.

We went some way to improving on her back, and she was pleased to feel improvements in the way of posture and co-ordination.
Still, even after this, *Otto* did not show any improvement. I was puzzled.
What was going on with him?

It was at that point that I had the idea of calling in my friend Linda. (She is the *spiritual healer* mentioned earlier in the book, who had introduced me to working with horses.)

She had worked with *Otto* and knew him well, and was very familiar with the yard he had come from.

I brought the idea up with Jane and asked if that would be okay with her, offering also to split my fee with Linda, so that there would be no extra cost to Jane.

She was more than a little sceptical of the term 'spiritual healing', but I suggested to her that no harm would come of it, and added that Linda was very astute and experienced, and might pick up on something I was not able to see.

What was there to lose?

Linda agreed quite readily to come to the yard, and the next week we were both standing in *Otto's* stable, with *Jane* watching.

Linda stood very still; 'tuning in' on *Otto*.....

(It is not my place to describe how Linda works, but it would be accurate to say that she works very much with colour, as these occur in the aura surrounding living beings. It is almost as if the 'emotional resonance' of that being, whether it is an animal or a

167

person, is present in the colours, and Linda has a very
accurate way of reading these colours...)

With her eyes closed, hands held a few inches over
the pony, *Linda* described *Otto's* colours as being dull
and listless. She said that he was fearful, that there
was the feeling of being 'trapped'....that his free spirit
was being suffocated, held in a vacuum…

Naturally, she tried as far as she could to be tactful, to
not come from an attitude of attack, or judgement
towards *Jane*. Unfortunately, it was clear that *Jane*
did not appreciate *Linda's* view of the pony's state. In
fact, she was only able to accompany me on one
further visit to *Otto*, before I was asked to 'come
alone'.

Linda has since told me more about those visits to
Otto. She says that in addition to her picking up his
feelings of being 'trapped and suffocated, as if he was
caught in a vacuum', she felt his *'sense of panic at*
being asked to perform at a very exacting standard,
one of perfectionism: If you do things well, you will be
rewarded, otherwise you can expect to be punished'.

After this, the vet was called in, and the pony's legs
were bandaged and he was medicated for laminitis.

I was not asked back to that yard, and lost touch until
the day I had a call from *Linda* to ask me if I knew
that *Otto* had been put to sleep…

Apparently, she had tried to rescue *Otto*, after a
panicked call from his original owner, who had heard
of *Jane's* intention to be rid of the pony.

'What can I do?' she asked,' I should never have sold
Otto to her!'

At the eleventh hour, *Linda* called *Jane* and begged
for his life. She offered to buy *Otto*; she would retire
him to a field where she would simply allow him to
quietly live out the rest of his days. Just being himself.

Jane refused. In fact she was quite abusive toward
Linda, feeling that, as the owner of the pony, she had
every right to do as she chose with him.

Otto was put to sleep.

There is more to it. A little while after this, *Jane*
called *Otto's* original owner to ask her whether she
would loan her another of her ponies called *Treasure*,
to keep *Jane's* surviving pony company. She was
persuasive enough to make it happen.

*Treasure immediately developed laminitis, he had
never had it before!*

When *Linda* heard about this from *Treasure's* worried owner, she immediately accompanied her to the yard. *Treasure* lay there in her stable, sad and disconsolate, unable and unwilling to get up.

What she heard from that pony was: *'Please, help me! Get me out of here!'*

She says that, at that point she could feel the presence of *Otto* there, urging her to save his old friend.

She acted without hesitation; she and *Treasure's* owner loaded him straight into the horsebox and took him home. The pony recovered within days.

What can we learn from this distressing story?

We have seen the image of a horse being moulded into 'being a good boy', and we see that horses are horses and cannot; will not be humans. (We see the taking of afternoon tea, where a pony is being persuaded to be more like a human.)

We see the damage done by over-expectation and perfectionism.

It is not my intention to stand in judgement of anyone involved here, and I ask the reader to forgive me if I come over in that way. We all try to do the best we can, given our limitations.

170

I have tried to present the facts as they occurred, even though it all happened several years ago, my friend Linda became extremely upset when I asked her to recount the details.

She feels, as I do, that Otto's story needs to be told; that the story of his tragic passing might teach others, in the telling of it, to become more sensitive to the needs of animals, *as animals*.

Chapter Twenty-Two: *'Spookiness'*....

Inevitably, doing the sort of work I do, I come up against those who feel threatened in some way by this healing work.

Why do they feel threatened?

I can only guess why this would be. I have to remind myself that it is neither my responsibility nor my business what people *think* of my work or me, but it does upset me if a horse is unable to receive a healing due to the owner's reluctance to try something a little different.

Sometimes people are just not ready for it.

I believe that in some cases this reluctance might be due to a sense of misplaced *religiousness*. As in:

'Are you coming from God or from the devil?'

It can be hard for some people to include this kind of healing in their belief systems. From where they are, they might feel that their faith precludes acceptance of something not specifically endorsed by doctrine.

In others, there is a lack of scientific validation in healing/intuitive work, not compatible with the current scientific mindset. As in:

'Can you prove that this actually works?'

Understandably:

Most forms of healing are neither explicable nor provable in conventional, scientific terms.

Not yet, anyway…

And yet, the improvement in most cases is clear to see. After more than ten years of being a Horse Listener, I have yet to see a horse manifest any negative side effects from my 'ministrations'.

I have included a couple of examples to illustrate the problem, what a friend of mine calls *'the problem of Spookiness'.*

The year I started out treating horses, I visited a yard, and because I was there for the first time, went to the house to announce myself.

The person who answered the door was the groom. She told me that the owner of the horse was out, but was about to return home.

There was something strange about her, and she seemed to get stranger when I said I was there to treat a horse. She would not meet my eyes.

Anyway, I went out to the yard and was met there almost immediately by the owner. All went well, and I returned a week later to find the horse much improved. As I was leaving, the owner said: *'By the way, my groom thinks you are the Devil!'* It turned out that this poor frightened groom had been diagnosed as a schizophrenic; who knows what she was seeing!

Here's where it gets stranger:

I returned to that yard some time later, to see to a new horse. Again I went to the house to announce myself. This time I was met at the door by the cleaner. I told her who I was, and that I was there to heal a horse. Her eyes widened.

Later, as I was leaving, the owner said: *'By the way, my cleaner thinks you are Jesus!'*

What can one say? The Devil or Jesus?

Well, you could say, people only see themselves. Or you could say that people pick up something different about you, they sense something about your *energy*, which is …unusual. Then they fall back on their belief-systems to help them out with explaining things. Belief-systems can fall short of adequate information, then people like me become *'spooky'*. One can't imagine how hard it was for the healers, herbalists and holy men and women of the middle-ages…..

I will mention another example to show *the problem of spookiness,* as regards the possible triggering of emotions dormant in others

Going back some years now, I made several regular visits to a yard nearby, where there is a wonderful team of carriage-horses.

These working horses are enormous, and they work in pairs, hitched to carriages of various kinds, including a hearse!

They are hired out for weddings and special functions requiring something more special and traditional, and even for the occasional funeral.

To accompany the horses and carriages, there are liveried coachmen dressed resplendently in red and black. It is a wonderfully stirring sight to see them go by, the horses trotting proudly in their black leather harnesses, encrusted with jewels and polished brass...

Over a period of some months I got to know these beautiful horses, each one hand picked and trained meticulously for the job.

It is hard to tell one member of a pair from the other, so well are they matched. They are even named to suggest their working partnerships.

One pair might be *'Laurel and Hardy'*, *'Benson and Hedges'* another….

I would attend to at least four pairs of these horses, some grey, some chocolate brown, almost black.

The owner/manager of this yard, whom I shall call G, was very happy with my work and the positive effect it had on the horses, and I loved visiting there.

It goes without saying that her livelihood depended on the horses being in perfect health, and she felt that my *healing work* with them was an important contribution.

G's border terrier grew quite fond of me and would run off to find little gifts for me when I arrived. One day she would offer a half-chewed apple, another day a piece of dusty rope…little treasures from the yard, given with love!

On one occasion this dear little dog even leapt into my arms from a moving car!

For a time all went well with my regular visits to the yard, until one day when G hurt her back after a fall from a horse. She called in to see me at my clinic. Something happened there, which subsequently curtailed my visits to her yard:

Immediately after her treatment, she became very emotional and burst into tears before she could begin to control the flood.

I think this shook her and clearly took her by surprise, She was not expecting a release at *that level* of her being and neither was I.

What she had expected was simply relief from the pain of spasmed muscles, and what she got was a whole lot more.

It is my belief that a lot of sustained emotional stress, lurking just under the surface, found an opportunity to release, and poor G was not ready for that...

She then became fearful and somehow threatened.

She had not meant to let me see a part of her own emotional self, which she had kept shut away so carefully from everyone.

Even from herself.

As concerned and as careful as I might be, I cannot take responsibility for a healing response, or reaction; I generally caution people about these healing reactions.

In the case of horses, I always advise a day of rest after a healing,

With no riding or strenuous work.

Whatever my theories might be on her
response/reaction, it was, effectively, the end of my
visits to G's yard for a while,
They have only recently recommenced, after a gap of
some years.
There have been others, who like G, were put off by
their own strong reactions to healing.
Or simply projected their own fears outward, onto
me…
There is an expression, which aptly describes the
process:

*'Love brings up anything unlike itself for the purpose
of release'*

Chapter Twenty-Three: *'The House in the Woods'*

Some of my earliest and most pleasant experiences in this field were visits to *'The House in the Woods'*, in *Surrey*.

There I would meet with a friendly and enthusiastic *Jenny H*, who would present to me a variety of dogs and horses for treatment.

Amongst these was *Desi*, a grey gelding, who had an unusual personality and a problem with his back that I could just never quite seem to get to the bottom of (no pun intended)…It was something intermittent. It was there one day and gone the next.

Desi was always friendly and cooperative, and would settle down and relax as soon as I put my hands on him.

Being a very tactile horse, I think he enjoyed the contact. And he loved the company of humans. He was one of those who made my early experiences with horses pleasant and memorable.

Solo was another character, as unusual in his own way as *Desi*, but decidedly more eccentric. You got the feeling he liked to think he was in charge. If you *didn't* get that feeling, he would make sure you did. How? You would get *bitten. Gently. Playfully.*

Solo suffered from back problems, and I saw him on and off over a couple of years. I learned to duck his playful teeth. Mostly.

I have a photograph of him staring into the sky, tracking a helicopter.

That was typical of *Solo*.

Most horses *never* look up at the sky. (neither, for that matter, do people)

He did. He took an interest in *everything* going on about him.

After all, he was in charge.

Purdy was one of my more difficult clients there. She suffered from ongoing hormonal problems, and was bad tempered when in season. And boy did she let you know it!

At these times she would kick out ferociously at anything. Moving or not moving. Even the walls of her box .I remember that August was her bad month. *Jenny* had to line her stable with rubber walling. She

180

called it the *'hock-proof box'*. She was convinced that this behaviour was *Purdy's 'self sabotage' routine*. This was the mare's way of ensuring that she was left alone. I have been asked *not* to mention the incident at Windsor…

In contrast to *Purdy* was the delightful *Floozy*.

Aptly named, she would show affection to almost *anyone* in the yard, be they stallion, gelding or person. Particularly when she was in season.

Although she did not always come up to expectation as an eventer, she provided amusement in the stable yard, certainly to me.

She was also very receptive to the *healing energies* working through my hands, showing some of the biggest yawns I have ever seen! (yawns are, for me, one of the signs that the *healing energies* are making positive changes in the horse)

Gypsy, an ancient chocolate-coloured pony, was another venerable client.

She had a certain dignity about her, a kindness.

This was a gentle soul, one of the oldest ponies in the yard, having seen *Jenny's* daughter from childhood to adulthood.

Treating her was rather like treating the matriarch of the yard,
The Grandmother or *Elder*.
In her were the memories of every event in that yard,
the whisperings of ponies and horses passing through,
telling of the ups and downs of daily life.
Her passing, some years later, was a sad event for the family:
She is sorely missed.

At *'The House in the Woods'* I treated several ponies, horses and dogs over a period of some years.
Naturally I built up relationships there, with *Jenny*, her family, and the horses and dogs. Conversation there was always interesting and informative. I learned a lot about horses and their behaviour.
This yard was clean and well kept; no expense was spared on those beloved creatures, no problem was left unsolved!

Another strong personality at *'The House in the Woods'* was a dog called *Puffer*.
She loved to spend time digging into the dung heap, looking for mice, rats, or whatever she imagined was living in there.

She would often trot up to me, her snout dusty with her labours, as if to assert her dominance in the yard, as if to show who was *really* in charge there.

One day *Jenny* asked me if I would treat *Puffer*, as she seemed to have some problems walking, it seemed to be originating from her back.

Puffer was a bit wary, only allowing me to work on her for a few minutes.

Then she scampered off, actually hiding under the bushes from me!

I waited, knowing she'd be back.

Sure enough, she eventually emerged from her hiding spot, trotted up to me,

Staring up at me, as if to say: "

'Okay, I'm ready for you now. I can just about fit you into my busy schedule, so hurry up and get on with it, won't you?'

Puffer only recently passed away, after a long and beloved life.

There will never be another like her.

Flora, the other dog in that yard, is a sleek black *Labrador*,

Always friendly and up for some fun!

I have continued to treat her over some years, for a variety of problems, ranging from stiff muscles and joints, to other more emotional issues, including the passing of her master, who would often take her out hunting with him.

She clearly missed him terribly, and took a long time to accept his absence.

Flora has become a great friend, and treating her is also like catching up and having a chat.

I know she enjoys the healing sessions; she makes it known in her *Labrador* way. She lets me know when her session is over, when she's had enough. Usually she will raise a front paw or roll onto her back, legs in the air.

I think the object of writing this particular chapter is to show how building a relationship in a yard creates a stronger connection, one of continuity and trust: Where the animals see you as a part of their lives, a part of their normality.

Also, it is another tribute to the many things I have learned from animals and people on my regular visits, especially to *'The House in the Woods'*.

What seems to happen is rather like the process of osmosis: things are absorbed invisibly into the skin,

184

learned in ways not grasped by the usual avenue of the senses.

There is a communion of souls, a whispering *one-sciousness..*

Allowing a relationship to develop over time is a bonus and is unusual in this work, since many of my treatments are *'one-offs'*, where one session suffices or where clients *'taste the product'*, so to speak, establishing whether or not they resonate with it; whether its something they are comfortable with, or not.

At the *'House in the Woods'* I found my confidence, partly because I was treated with respect and friendliness, and partly because the animals were treated in just the same way.

Jenny, in her own natural and instinctive way, would let me into her world; sharing with me her insights into the personalities of the animals.

I was never treated as a *'beginner'*, even though I clearly was, and that made an enormous difference to me, in trusting the healings.

Jenny is a very intuitive person who, over the years I have known her, has trusted and developed her inner powers of perception to the point of acute focus. Thank you, *Jenny* and all those other teachers at *'The House in the Woods'*.

Chapter Twenty-Four: *Roxy*

This *Arab* mare lay on her side on the floor of her
stall.

She looked tired, depressed.

I walked over to her, but stood off to one side of the
box out of respect for her vulnerable position. Giving
her a little space.

She laboriously struggled to her feet.

This was an effort, a huge effort, as if she did not
want to get up at all,

As if she did not want to be there at all.

Her eyes were dull, sunken; her coat lacklustre.

She had the look of a horse that had given up on
herself, with very little will to live.

Her owner, who deeply loves her, covered in brief the
history of *Roxy's* demise.

At some point, after a promising beginning, she had
developed a problem in her left foreleg, which had
swollen up and refused to heal.

The vet had finally injected the knee joint with a steroid.

Immediately after this she went lame in all four legs, unable to stand comfortably. She took to lying down most of the time on the floor of her box.

The vet's diagnosis at this point was *laminitis*.
Box rest was prescribed, but made no difference.
Even after several weeks.
In fact, things got worse, her owner began to lose heart.

The vet felt that he could do no more for the mare: it was a hopeless case.
He suggested to the owner that she put *Roxy* down.
At this point I was called in.

After my first session, *Roxy* did not show much response, but she clearly enjoyed the flow of energy moving through my hands. She settled into it; head drooping, eyes closed.

Following on the second session, her owner reported a sudden and distinct change for the better:

Roxy was now more alert; keen on her food, more comfortable overall and even happy to stand, for periods of time, on her feet.

She was no longer lying for hours on her side on the floor of stable.

There was now a shine in her eyes, a lift in her spirits.

Following her third visit she showed so much improvement that she was let into the field, where she was actually seen cantering about!

This was unthinkable three weeks before.

Roxy was beginning to enjoy life again.

Although her owner has said that she will never ride her again, she seems content to keep her as a pet, as a retired horse.

There are some who see this change in her as miraculous.

Others are rather more sceptical, wanting to see *more*, wanting to see her return to eventing.

This does not seem to be part of the *'plan'*.

I returned to that yard some weeks later.

There was *Roxy*, out grazing in the field. I went over and leaned on the wooden fence. *Roxy* came trotting over to me, her ears forward.

She approached me and nuzzled my shoulder playfully.

We met eyes.

Connected.

I felt her strength, returned.

I felt her feistiness, restored.

Roxy was back.

Chapter Twenty-Five: *'The White Horse'*

By now you should be getting some idea of the kind
of approach I bring to what I call *'horse listening'*.
And hopefully, with it, some understanding
The *Intuitive* nature of this work; as demonstrated
through many different examples, will shine through.
I make no claims to infallibility. What I do does not
always work; neither does it work for *every* horse or
every problem. It is but one form of *healing*. I freely
admit that in many respects I am still learning, still
striving to bring focus to it.
All is *'through a glass darkly'*,
All is limited by my own perspective.

I was going to leave out this part of the book,
But it keeps popping into my head with such
insistence,
I finally decided to go with it.
So here it is:

I must now introduce an *invisible friend.*

One who remains a constant guide to me in my work.

One whom I admit, I tend to take for granted.

My wife Debra, who was born with the gift of
clairvoyance;

Was shocked one day on my return home from my
horse rounds.

She saw me walk into our living room followed by a
white horse,

More correctly, a *'Spirit Horse'*.

She has seen this guide with me several times since,

And I have become increasingly aware of its presence,

In my work with horses and other animals.

On one occasion I was attending to a difficult mare,
which was given to biting.

Suddenly she noticed something standing alongside
me, showed the whites of her eyes and backed off into
a corner of the stable.

She was seeing The White Horse.

She was, from that moment, on her best behaviour,
throwing occasional glances to my right side.

I am confident that, notwithstanding being careful and
respectful of the animal's space; *'The White Horse'* is
always at my side to protect and guide me.

Perhaps the information given to me is conveyed through this Spirit:

I am open to further insights in this regard.

What I have become aware of, more and more, is that there are helpful and benign Energies at work whenever I am doing this healing work. It would be fair, respectful, and appropriate to acknowledge their influence.

Although they are invisible to me, I can feel their radiance, their energies.

Angels have been described by every religion, every cult, over millennia.

The Greek word 'angelos', means messenger. These are messengers from higher realms, from realms of light.

Spiritual Healers speak of their 'guides', I have heard them describe how they look, and they quite often have specific names.

I believe that The White Horse is such a being.

A guide. An angel. A helpful friend from the spirit world, sent to bring healing to the animals.

Chapter Twenty-Six: *Ollie and the pink pyjamas.*

I was recently asked to attend to a gelding called
Ollie.
Sharon, his owner, called me and said that he had a
few issues.
Firstly, *Ollie* was not at all happy about being saddled.
What really annoyed him, she said, was having the
girth straps tightened.

Her trainer, *Cheryl*, who is mentioned elsewhere in
this book as the owner of *Erika* and of *Krumpet* the
rescued racehorse, had applied the *'Join up'* (*Monty
Roberts) Method* in an attempt to overcome the
problem with his saddle.
This technique is useful in creating closer bonds
between rider and horse and I have seen its
effectiveness in overcoming irrational fears in horses,
such as shying away from flapping plastic bags, and
refusing to enter a trailer.

But even after *Join up*, *Ollie* was no closer to
accepting a saddle on his back.

194

In addition to this, there was a general attitude
problem:

He was always grumpy, putting his ears back and
showing his teeth.

So, having been acquainted with some of his issues, I
arrived at *Ollie's* yard on a freezing cold winter's day.
Being on the crest of a hill intensified the wind-chill
factor still more.

It was already getting dark, and I agreed to treat *Ollie*
outside, as *Sharon* had mentioned his nervousness in
the stable, particularly with strangers.

I sensed his dislike for being touched, so I spent just a
few minutes with my hands on him, then made an
appointment for a later date.

Ollie was clearly a complex case.
That was already obvious.
In addition to what I had been told about him, he had
already been moved several times, and *Sharon* was
dealing with some difficult emotional issues of her
own, including the death of her mother.

This would only add to *Ollie's* own emotional baggage.

With the next visit, I was confident enough to ask *Sharon* to let me treat him in his stable. Once again, it was another bitterly cold day outdoors on that exposed hilltop!

This time, knowing *Ollie's* sensitivity to touch, *I held my hands some distance away from his body, not actually making physical contact.*

His response to this was immediate, his head lowered and be began to lick and chew (classic responses which show willingness, responsiveness.), and then to yawn and stretch his neck.

Holding my hands over his posterior, I sensed that there was an old injury held in the muscles of the right lumbar and hip area.

Acting on a hunch, I then reached over and held my hand just above the area around his left shoulder. Again, Ollie showed a similar response.

This confirmed for me that the problem was a long-standing one, as I will routinely find that lower back tensions will transfer to the opposite shoulder, by way of the body compensating for the tension there.

196

At this point *Sharon* mentioned that he had *'old issues'* with his right hip, which had been injured when he was with his previous owners.

All of this had obviously contributed to *Ollie's* discomfort, his overall unhappiness with life. He was stiff and in pain.

Then, just as I completing that session, I clearly heard him say:

'I'm cold, tell her I'm cold; I could do with a nice warm blanket'

Really?

'Yes, really!

'

I told *Sharon* straight off what *Ollie* had *'whispered'* to me.

She was amazed.

So was I. It had taken me by surprise.

I also told her what I had found in his back and shoulder. I said that, with the tight muscles in his back having irritated the nerves over time, it was likely that *Ollie's* skin had become hypersensitive, which was why he was not happy about being saddled.

And why he was so cold.

She lost no time: that same afternoon *Ollie* was cosily fitted with a soft pink fleecy blanket.

Sharon said that from the moment the pink fleece was put on him, *Ollie* relaxed and showed an immediate improvement in attitude.
He became more easy-going and responsive.
No wonder!
He didn't have to expend all his energy fighting the cold!

With my next session, I found I was able to place my hands directly on *Ollie's* body without a reaction from him.
Now I was able to work deeply into those tightly splinted shoulder muscles.
The lumbar and hip area had already improved since the last visit,
Ollie was now actually enjoying the contact, showing complete trust in it.

I have seen *Ollie* about three months since that last session,

Sharon has moved him to a yard where he has been reunited with an old friend, a horse formerly owned by *Sharon's* daughter.

The change in *Ollie* is remarkable. He is contented with his life; I found no trace of the old injury in his right hind. He is no longer sensitive to the touch, except for an area in the left shoulder, which will still need a little more of my attentions. He goes out with complete willingness on his hacks with *Sharon* and helped to bring about a positive change in *Sharon* herself.

Thinking back on him, though, he was certainly a fine figure of a horse on that windswept hilltop, happy and warm in his new *pink pyjamas!*

Chapter Twenty-Seven: Other tools: *Energy Psychology and Josh.*

Around seven years ago my wife *Debra* and I went to *San Diego, California* to undertake some intensive training in *Energy Psychology.*

We both felt drawn to learning more about these new tools for healing, having seen some very effective demonstrations of it back home.

It is not my intention to showcase the various forms of this experimental process in this book, since there are by now many different types of *energy psychology*, which are far more comprehensively described elsewhere by leaders in that field *(Fred Gallo, Gary Craig and others.)*

Put in the simplest way, *energy psychology* works like this:

Negative emotions, fears or traumas; particularly if they have been held for a long period of time, can be re-experienced each time a similar event comes up to trigger it,

Rather like a recurring pattern of behaviour.

Energy Psychology addresses these patterns of negative emotional reaction.

It reduces that negative emotional reaction, often eradicating it altogether.

This is done without any negative side-effects, it is completely safe, and often 100% effective.

It has two components:

First is to hold the memory of the trauma, (or negative emotion) in the mind and to rate it's intensity on a 'subjective scale of distress',

Then tapping on specific points, also known as acupressure points, on the body, in a certain pattern called an 'algorithm', whilst constantly repeating a statement that describes the trauma or negative emotion.

It is an elegant and easily taught technique that anyone can learn to do.

Debra and I learned at least three different, but related techniques,

Specifically designed for dealing with issues ranging from fears to phobias,

Depression to low self esteem, addiction to eating disorders.

Whilst there, I met one or two people who had adapted the techniques of energy psychology for use on animals.

Over the years I am finding *energy psychology, or 'tapping',* increasingly useful for dealing with issues shared by rider and horse.

Here is an example:

Kate asked me if there was something I could do for a problem she was having with her horse, *Josh*.

At some time in the past she had been show jumping, and *Josh* had stopped up short, refusing to take the jump.

This had created extreme anger in her, and anxiety in the *Josh*, who was picking up her anger.

Every time she approached a jump afterward, she would encounter the same emotional resistance, the same trauma; shared by her and *Josh*.

Clearly this had become a persistent pattern,

Recurring each time a jump was approached.

Initially I treated *Josh* in my usual way, finding some muscle tension in his right lumbar spine, and also shoulders and neck.

Then I felt that, since he and *Kate* were sharing the
trauma or anxiety;
That *energy psychology* might be useful in clearing
the pattern.

So I asked *Kate* to hold the memory of that first
trauma with *Josh*,
To really feel the anger,
To really recall the frustration of that failed attempt at
the jump;
Then, whilst *tuning in* to that strongly negative
emotion,
We *tapped* on specific points, *acupressure points*,
In a sequence called an *'algorithm'*.

Almost immediately *Kate* burst into tears,
Releasing the anger and frustration held so long in her
emotional body.
This surprised her; she had not known how strong she
had felt all that time,
And now she was feeling incredibly calm, even
elated.

Now we were going to apply the same technique on
her horse.

As we stood in *Kate's* yard, I asked her to place a hand on *Josh's* forehead, over the third eye. Simultaneously, I asked her to recall the traumatic incident as strongly as she could, remembering as much detail as possible.

The very next moment, the horse reacted by kicking out with his right rear leg.
His ears went back, he appeared to be re-experiencing that past event.
I tapped his *shoulder point* whilst *Kate* was re-living the memory,
Then, using a very experimental component of the technique
(Which is completely harmless),
I asked *Kate* to *surrogate*, to *'be'* Josh; once again, *tuning in* on the original traumatic memory.
Then I tapped *her* acupressure points, while she focussed on *'being'* Josh.
Once more, she initially felt some strong feelings come up;
But now she was doing this *as if she was Josh.*

Immediately after, she reported a sensation of calm and well-being.

Interestingly, *Josh* also relaxed straight away, nodding right off to sleep!

This has been a total success,

Rider and horse have now been fully put to the test.

What is also good to see is a closer bond between the two.

Friends have noticed a change in *Kate's* riding ability.

Some say she is more confident, but also more relaxed;

More outgoing, more at peace with herself.

Josh has more energy and is better coordinated.

He is more trusting, less anxious.

In another example of the *energy psychology* approach to horse/rider problems, I found the following case worth mentioning:

Jan has been a client for several years now,

During that time I have treated several of her horses with different kinds of issues ranging from stiffness, to behavioural problems.

Recently we used the energy psychology approach on a couple of her horses, including a mare called *Marty*.

Jan has done a course in *'EFT'*, one of the *energy psychology* techniques formulated by *Gary Craig*, and so she needed no introduction to all of this.

Standing with *Jan* in *Marty's* stable, I become aware of just how sensitive the mare is:

It is almost hyperactive. It can't or won't relax.

I lay my hands on *Marty* to calm her down.

Jan, holding her head collar, is a little anxious.

The mare has a reputation for being difficult at times.

She can be skittish, has been known to bite.

So I proceed with a little healing.

Finally, she seems calmer, less fidgety.

At this point I tap lightly on her shoulder points,

In front of and behind the foreleg, where it meets the shoulder.

Then, I ask *Jan* to be the *surrogate* for *Marty*.

This is done by lightly tapping a certain area of the head in an arc just above the ear; whilst saying, *'I am Marty'*

Yes, I know it sounds bizarre, but it works!

So *Jan* applied this procedure and I worked through the *algorithm* with her,

As if she was the mare.

After completing the sequence, we reached a point where we reversed the surrogate tapping, *bringing Jan back to herself.* However, things did not go as well as I had hoped.

Somehow the impression of being *Marty* was too strong for *Jan,*

She phoned me up the following week to say that for that night,

Following the treatment, she had pains in her body that were *'new'*;

She felt that she had taken on *Marty's* problems,

She said it was a weird, uncomfortable feeling.

She felt tension in her right hip,

Her neck and shoulders,

As if she was *'twisted'.*

These were pretty much the areas I had found with the *mare.*

It has be said, though, and *Jan* would agree,

That she is more empathic than most;

More likely to pick up what is going on with her horses.

This is very similar to the experience of clairsentience,

Described in chapter seventeen of this book;

Where I made mention of *Mary* and *Magic*,

As examples of this kind of experience.

It was a disturbing experience for *Jan*;

However, it was very temporary:

She was fine the next day and the mare was more relaxed with her.

My first commitment in this work is help the horse as much as possible.

Whether it is simply a matter of releasing muscle tension,

Going a little deeper into restoring the flow of energy,

Or recognizing behavioural issues from the past and clearing them.

Or seeing that there are things for the rider to take responsibility for,

Such as addressing their own back problems;

And releasing shared traumas with their horses:

Adding tools such as energy psychology has widened the possibilities,

But the goal remains the same:

Restoring wellness intuitively,

To achieve Wholeness,

One-sciousness

Chapter Twenty-Eight: *Reactions, Reports and Responses.*

Although, by now, I have covered many different kinds of problems in many different kinds of horses; there are some responses and reactions that are similar and are worth covering here.

They are also, I think, interesting.

Sometimes I will not hear from the owners of horses, but will have them call me much later to report on their progress, which is often dramatic.

When I start out with a healing session, I see:

1. *Drooping neck and lips, with eyes closing.*
2. *Yawning, with neck stretching.*
3. *Twitching of skin and underlying muscle.*
4. *Deep sighing.*
5. *Dropping off to sleep.*

There are, of course, combinations of the above, and sometimes no detectible response at all, even though

there may well have been some changes or
adaptations, as I like to call them.

Mostly common is the gradual lowering of the head,
and the drooping lips.
I find that this is a comforting confirmation that the
horse is feeling the healing energies and responding to
them.
In addition to this, the horse will quite often turn an
ear in my direction, paying attention to an area which
might need healing.

When I am working at the level of tight, splinted
muscles;
I will often find the animal's head and neck turn
toward the area, affirming that this is where the
problem is.
Obviously, if there is pain or discomfort there,
The horse will register this as a flattening of the ears,
or a movement indicating displeasure.
This is where I need to watch and listen, acting in
response to the animal's reactions.
Sometimes a horse will register pain or discomfort
when I am working at the level of muscles, especially
if it has suffered a sprain or strain, *by making as if it is*

about to bite me. This would apply to any animal in pain. In rare cases, where I have not being paying enough attention, where I've not *got the* message, I have been bitten. In one instance I had managed to get myself wedged between a fractious mare and her hay net. Her ears were back and she was giving me the signals! Still I didn't move. Then she bit me to persuade me that I should move away from her food source! I got this impressive bite on the cheek which drew blood. It was more a case of hurt pride than real injury, *'I mean, I was only trying to help you out, you ungrateful mare!'*

Lesson learned: don't get between a hungry horse and it's hay-bag!

So, yes, one learns to read the signals and reactions…Overall, though, I have had very little in the way of aggressive response from horses. They know when you are there to help them, they sense it, and they are willing to cooperate. I have had to actually *'withdraw from the field of action!'* on only two occasions. This is one of them:

One day I was called out to see a stallion. The owner was a teenage girl called *Beccy*. She spoke to me over the phone, I remember that she was very emotional, tearful. She said that her horse had become very aggressive toward everyone except her, and that she did not want her mother to know that I was seeing the horse. She was afraid that he might be taken from her.

I agreed to meet her at the yard. When I arrived there I was met by a man who introduced himself as *Beccy's* stepfather. *Something immediately registered as I shook his hand, call it a tickle of the intuitive antennae.*

Beccy arrived a moment later with the stallion, whom she had brought in from the field. He was big, angry and not happy about being brought in. As I stepped forward toward him, his ears went back and he showed me the whites of his eyes. Not a good sign! I noticed a quick exchange between *Beccy* and her stepfather. What did it mean, and why was I feeling so disturbed by it? She was an attractive girl, and the look between them was secretive, almost guilty. I returned my attention to the stallion. Just in time too, he was raising a hind leg in readiness for kicking a horse-listener into touch!

Still I approached, near enough to lay a hesitant hand on his back. It was as if I had poked him with a sharp stick. He exploded into a kick (which missed) then reared up, flailing his forelegs and showing his teeth. I looked over at *Beccy*. Her face was streaked with tears; she was struggling to settle the stallion, talking to it, holding onto the head collar. He responded to her, gradually calming down, but now flicking his tail from side to side, showing his annoyance. Once again, I slowly approached him from the left flank. He did not respond. I *very, very* gently laid hands on his back, just over the withers and the sacrum. I could feel muscles knotted like steel wires. His skin twitched, but *Beccy* spoke softly in his ear. For around five minutes there was some calm, I felt him beginning to relax…Then I signalled to *Beccy* that the session was over. She led the stallion out into the field and I watched as the stallion took off, bucking and galloping about, like a thing possessed. To me, this was not just high-spiritedness, this was a disturbed animal…

I set an appointment for a week later and left the yard. Driving away in my car, I watched the two in my mirror. *Beccy* and her stepfather. Something not quite healthy there, I felt. Still. Not my place to judge. But that stallion…could I really help him? Can but try..

Two days later *Beccy* phoned to cancel the appointment. Would the following week be okay?

Sure, I said. How was the stallion, I asked? She burst into tears. I waited for her to become intelligible. She said she didn't really know, but the vet had refused to treat him, he said the stallion was crazy, a danger to everyone, that it should be put down…

I arrived at the yard to find things just as they had been two weeks before. This time the stepfather was not there. Once more, same pattern of behaviour: the threatening hooves, the whites of the eyes, the rearing up and the flailing of forelegs. This time, I did not get a chance to lay a hand on this disturbed horse. He came straight at me. But for *Beccy's* quick thinking I would have had some flying lessons. She pulled on his head-collar, deflecting the attack from me, and allowing me to retreat to a safe distance, behind the fence! She was very upset. I could see what was going through her mind. The vet would not help, declaring her horse insane; now she could see that I was not able to reach through the turmoil in her stallion's mind, not able to reach a place where I could bring peace..

She turned him out and came to where I was at the fence. She was crying.

She knew what I was about to say. *'Sorry Beccy, I cannot treat your horse, it's just too dangerous.'* She tearfully nodded, silently leading the stallion away. I wanted to say more. I wanted to offer something, comforting words. I wanted to ask her if things were okay at home, if she wanted to talk about it…

Instead, I stood quietly watching her walk into the field with the stallion. There was nothing more I could say or do.

I offer this as an extreme example of a horse I could not treat. Perhaps, you might say, it may have been possible to do more, under sedation. Possibly.

At the time, my intuitions advised me to walk away. There was more to it than just a seriously disturbed horse.

Happily, I have only ever had positive responses, aside from those exceptions. Amongst the reports I have received are these: *'The mare is behaving herself now, she's enjoying her life'*

'He seems years younger, he's as cheeky as a youngster'

'Her appetite has improved and her coat looks healthier'

'Before you treated him, he was sluggish and unwilling to go out. Now, he greets me as I arrive at the yard, and he can't wait to go out'

'She seemed a little moody the day after you treated her, but now she is as bright as a button. I feel like she's come back to me…'

'I can definitely do more with him now, and the grooms have noticed how much happier he is now.'

'He's like a new horse. I don't recognize him from how he was before!'

These are just a few of the typical responses I have recorded, over the years.

The only 'negative' reactions reported to me are those that have to do with the horse's response to a healing. These are, typically, one of the following, or sometimes a combination of them:

1. Stiffness for a day or two after (as tight muscles release)

2. Moodiness, again only for a short time. (emotional releasing)

3. A sudden abundance of energy.

4. Changes in behaviour, always for the better.

Horses I have not been able to help *at all* are
invariably those that have some kind of serious,
undiagnosed illness; structural damage (to the skeletal
system), or serious mental problems.

Usually the vet would have detected these, and so it is
rare for me to encounter any of the above. On the
other hand, I have been known to be somewhat
cavalier, and say to someone who is not sure if I can
help: *'Let's give it a try, it can do no harm!'*
Miracles are always possible....

Chapter Twenty-Nine: *The foal that nearly wasn't*

For some years I have been paying regular visits to a
working yard,
Run by *Georgia* and her mother *Ali*.
They take horses and eventing very seriously; it is
their livelihood.
I find it is a wonderful place to visit:
The horses are kept fit and healthy and there is an
atmosphere of cheerful hard work. Nothing is spared
on these horses to maintain them,
So when I am called in, it is a pleasure to be informed
of each horse and what is seen to be amiss. Both *Ali*
and *Georgia* are very intuitive, and have a sense, an
understanding for what I do.

I could probably fill a book with the many instances
of horses and ailments we have dealt with at their
yard. They understand about regular maintenance on
horses too, so its not always *dramatic traumatic!*

One case I will cover here is that of their amazing foal called *Rocket*.

Georgia called me one day and briefed me:

Rocket, at that stage barely a yearling, had developed a case of enteritis.

The vet had been called in and after monitoring the situation over a number of days, had prescribed a course of antibiotics. This had helped, but the flora in the little foal's gut were left massively challenged by the effects of the antibiotic.

Then more medication was prescribed, but still the problems continued.

Georgia was finally put in the position of having to decide whether she was going to keep *Rocket* or have him put down. She could see that he was a little fighter, no way was he going to give up!

This was the point at which she called me.

'Could you come in and maybe assess the situation? A decision has to be made.'

Already the foal had outlived all projected expectations of his demise. Most advice had been to put him down.

So I arrived at the yard to find this plucky foal
wobbling on spindly legs;
Skin stretched painfully over ribs, but with a fire in
his eyes.
Life asserting it's right to be: I gently laid hands on
him.
At first, I guess in anticipation of some scary medical
procedure,
(He'd had a few)
He shied away a little; then settled down as he felt the
energies moving through him.
In a short while he gave me a sign that things were
done; that the healing was completed.
I had this absolute certainty that the foal would live,
and I told *Georgia* my thoughts. She was pleased. She
had spent many anxious hours with the little foal,
there was a real love between them.

Today *Rocket* is alive and well,
Although he now has a new malady, he seems, as
usual, to be working through it.

I have another enduring picture in my mind from this
yard,
One I feel I would like to share:

I was standing in the stable of a wonderful grey called
Gypsy,
Known as *Gyp* to those who know and love him.
Gyp has a long-term malady, which affects the right
hind. With regular treatment the problem is
controlled.
He is a wonderfully willing, big-hearted eventer;
always giving of his best, always sweet of nature.

So I'm in the stable with *Gyp*,
But I'm not alone.
With me are two of *Ali's* granddaughters, and of
course, *Ali* herself.
I have just commenced treatment on the affable *Gyp*,
When *Ali* suddenly remembers something she has to
do in the next field.
So here's the picture:
She leaves the lead rope in the hands of the golden
haired *Sophie*, who, at three years old, has grown up
in this yard, and is happy to do this.
The other girl, *Katherine*, is just 6 months and lying,
for now, peacefully in her pram. Right there, in the
stable, alongside *Sophie*.

Gyp stretches his neck and affectionately nuzzles the baby on her cheek.

She giggles, the horse's soft lips tickling her cheek.

An idyllic scene.

Suddenly this heavenly moment is broken:

The baby notices *Ali* has left the stable:

She panics and starts to cry.

Loudly.

Very loudly.

Gyp seems a little tense.

Sophie, the three year old, tries to comfort her baby sister *Katherine.*

Unsuccessfully:

The decibel levels rise.

Sophie then decides, all at once, to go find *Ali*, leaving the lead rope, at this point, in the hands of her baby sister, *Katherine*, in the pram.

Get the picture?

It still makes me smile.

It really is wonderful to see children completely fearless around these big animals. I feel that is a picture of how things should be.

The innocence of children and animals.

Chapter Thirty: *The Driving Ponies*: *Anna and the 'Boys'.*

Early in my career as a *Horse Listener* I had a very pleasant association, for a couple of years, with *Anna* and her team of driving ponies.

Anna is an international competitor in this event and completely dedicated to the sport. She is a pleasant and sensitive woman, always endeavouring to do her best for her team of ponies, always looking for ways to get the best out of them without exploiting them. She is especially considerate of their feelings and energies. I have not come across many as caring as *Anna*.

The yard is immaculately clean, and as caring as *Anna* is, she is also a hard working and exacting person; expecting the same from her grooms.

Her ponies are chosen for many different qualities:
They must be the right size and have the right conformation,
They must be capable of working together as a team,

And they must be willing to work hard.
But most of all, they must enjoy working!

Anna travels the country to find suitable members for
her team.
Some of them are kept in reserve and gradually
trained,
Others become her stars in the team itself,
Or leaders if they show those qualities.
On my arrival in that busy, professional yard,
I would always be given a precise, amazingly detailed
report on the condition of each pony, as well as
indicators on where they might be having problems.
At that time I was still very green, very inexperienced.
I was eager to learn as much as possible about every
aspect;
It was great to be exposed to this kind of detail.

Using a combination of *BSR and energy work*, I was
always amazed at the response of these ponies. They
would settle down almost instantly that I laid hands
on them; into the now-familiar mode of receiving:
The drooping neck and head,
The half-closed eyes and floppy lips,
Almost falling asleep on their feet.

One or two would show an initial resistance,
especially if there were areas of tight muscle. Then, of
course, they might be quite sensitive to the touch;
sometimes even stiff and painful.

These ponies were wonderfully receptive creatures to
work with:
Small and well muscled, agile and intelligent.
Anna has only recently re-housed them all in
impressive new quarters,
After years of having to wrangle with the local
authority over planning permission to build the new
stables. At the time I treated the team, they were kept
in a wonderfully random and rambling collection of
small stables,
Interconnected by concrete walkways.
It was always exciting to find out how *Anna and her*
'boys', as she affectionately referred to them, had
been placed in their events.
Usually it would be in the top four.

Sometimes they would go across the channel to
France, and then the ponies would have to be issued
with travel documents or passports;
A concept that still tickles me!

Working with *Anna and the boys* was a great privilege to me,

Being so green, I was still unsure of the difference between *'withers'*, *'fetlocks'* and *'stifles'* and freely admit now that I had to pretend for a while that I did!

Anna saw each pony as having certain definite character traits,

After a while I began to see what she was seeing:

Perry was an outstanding performer, though at times, a little grumpy.

Rupert, the old man of the yard,

Demanded respect from the younger boys;

Happy was usually happy, but not always!

Sometimes I was given a little nibble,

But I would like to think it was out of affection!

Naturally, I found that the work I did in that yard was more muscle-based.

Physical rather than intuitive.

These were not ponies with behavioural problems or traumas from the past, Certainly not in the sense in which I treat horses with those problems today.

Anna is always careful when selecting ponies to find only the best, with caring and reputable owners.

I am sure *Anna* would not mind me mentioning that she got a certain pleasure at these events by beating quite regularly, *Prince Philip* himself, a keen and regular eventer. I hope *he* doesn't mind me mentioning this, though, I might end up in the *Tower of London…*!

Naturally, as these ponies have to not only negotiate some difficult courses,
Working as a coordinated team,
But they also have to be strong enough to carry a cart with two people in it.
They can end up with considerable stresses and strains.

I would usually find shoulder tensions,
Lower back tensions,
And sometimes joint strain.
Inasmuch as this is a competitive event,
The ponies can be considered athletes in their own right,
And they invariably have temperaments to match!

Anna would often describe just how the ponies,

The 'boys', would perform for their audience,

Becoming quite fierce and determined to take their

driver to victory.

They take their job very seriously.

This is a very specialised area in the horse-eventing

world,

And as I have mentioned before,

It was a great privilege to share in it for a time.

Some of these big-hearted little ponies have passed

on,

Since the days when I treated them.

Happy is still with *Anna*, I spoke to her just the other

day.

She was excited that she had sold some of her old

team to an American

Competitor,

Today, some eight years since I last saw her, she has a

completely new team,

And was last year placed fourth in the World

Championships.

She is now just as dedicated as ever she was.

I salute you, *Anna and the boys:*

Happy, Rupert, Poli, Perry, Picador, Peter, Star, and
Nibbs.

Chapter Thirty-One: *Mandy and Olympus.*

One of the first yards I worked in, with regularity,
Was that of *Mandy M*, who has since moved to
Cornwall.

Mandy is the niece of *Linda* (whom I have mentioned
before, as bringing me to this work and to my first
horse, *Lizzy*).

She is a wonderfully instinctive and intuitive person
with the horses in her yard, as well as the riders
involved with these horses.

It was always a great pleasure to have her input when
arriving there.

She owns a very sensitive and responsive horse, called
Olympus.

Mandy is a very emotional person, deeply connected
to animals.

For this reason she feels, in herself, what is going on
with them.

Although she was, at that time, a little lacking in self-
confidence;

She more than made up for it in terms of her intuitive
ability.

I treated many horses in her yard,
Over a period of some eight years, and I shall
mention, amongst them;
Cleo, Herman, Jazz, Chester and Stony;
Not forgetting the magnificent *Olympus*, about whom
more shall be said.

Also in that yard, as a fierce protector of *Mandy* and
her children was *Luke*,
Who is, sadly, no longer with us.
Luke was an Irish terrier, with the gentleness of a
dove,
And the heart of a lion.
He was also a 'patient' of mine, off and on, and a
great dog of great character.
He would always rush up to me in his fierce but
affectionate way,
Reminding me that he was the king, and required both
recognition and respect!

I remember one day conducting a session in that yard,
Still very experimental at that stage,

When a group of women standing around a horse I
was treating,
Suddenly felt the effects of the treatment it was
receiving!
They all reported a sensation of *'being transported
out of their bodies'*,
Of course, it was not well received by some!

One of that very group of ladies, *Elaine*, has since
gone on to become a Medical Intuitive;
But at that time she was not at all sure what she was
experiencing.
This is an example of how what we do has a knock-on
effect.
Something, someone we connect with at some point in
our lives,
Unknowingly, will influence us or spur us on to
something higher.

So there I was, at *Manor Livery*, *Mandy's* yard,
Treating *Olympus*, her dear horse-friend.
Olympus is and was a close member of her family:
He is very protective of her children and has a bond
with *Mark*, *Mandy's* husband, which is more human
than animal.

Mandy was feeling that she had been given the wrong sort of advice about *Olympus's* shoes from her farrier. The horse was just not able to give of his best, which in turn, was making him feel that he was letting her down. Her instincts were always sharp with him, right from the beginning. *Mandy* told me often that she felt this horse had been sent to her.

There was a connectedness of souls for her.

My first meeting with *Olympus* told me much the same:

This horse is meant to be with her.

Mandy has many years experience with horses and is a teacher/trainer,

Much respected in the riding fraternity.

Certainly I have not met with many as sensitive,

Or as intuitive about the horses she works with.

So now we had arrived at an impasse with *Olympus*:

Her vet could not offer any solution either, other than to suggest that the horse was not sound, which was a bit obvious!

On the other hand, *Mandy* has a tremendous loyalty to people,
And did not feel that she wanted to stand up to her farrier,
Whom she has used regularly for many years;
Or contradict his advice, even though she felt strongly that *Olympus* was wearing the wrong shoes…

Olympus is a gentle giant:
A strong horse with immense power,
But one who needs a caring and understanding rider,
in order to encourage the best out of him. *Mandy* always knew when he was out of sorts, or needing something.
On some occasions we would be standing in his stable together,
And she would, at those times, become emotional, or rather, connected emotionally to the horse; letting me know what she felt was going on with him.
We would usually concur, each in our different way.
Her instincts were always right, and yet (like so many of us),
She would not always trust those instincts.

The difficulty, quite often, is around the opinions of others, as well meaning as those might be. Someone once said:

'Opinion stands somewhere between ignorance and knowledge'

This might prove offensive to some, but there is sense in the fact that an opinion is still only an opinion.
One is as good as another, or as bad.
When tuning in to intuition, one tunes into an *inner knowingness:*
The more you trust it, the better it serves you.
And that inner knowingness does not always agree with the opinions of those around one. This is often a painful realization, and can lead to disagreements and even fallouts; the fact is though, that the inner voice has to be heard.
Mandy has learned to trust that inner voice, the voice of intuition, and it has certainly taught more than the opinions of others, however well-meaning they might be.

Chapter Thirty-Two: *Racehorses and egos.*

'Who the hell are you?'

'And what the hell are you doing here?'

'This is a racing yard, we don't allow just anyone in here!'

These words were bellowed from the mouth of a stocky red-faced man.

He stood opposite me, at the gate of the stable yard, arms akimbo.

He was clearly so angry at my intrusion that it looked as if a volcano was about to erupt out of the top of his head.

I answered, more than a little shocked:

'I'm expected here for an appointment at 4.15'

'I'm Peter Van Minnen'...

'I know that!', he responded,

'You're too early; take your car and get out of my yard!'

I couldn't believe this!

The last time someone had shouted at me like this was when I was serving compulsory military service, some thirty-five years previously in South Africa.

How rude!

My first impulse was to leave and never come back.

I didn't deserve this kind of treatment.

How dare he!

These adrenaline fuelled thoughts machine-gunned angrily through me as I climbed into my car and drove out of the yard.

'But wait!' said a restraining voice in my heated head, *'why should you give up on a horse you haven't even had the chance to treat yet?'*

'Also', the voice added, *'this rude man has nothing to do with your being called here.'*

'Just hang in there, buddy, you're bigger than that!'

(These are probably not the exact words, but, for the sake of drama, they'll do)

So I parked outside the gates and waited for the horse's owner to arrive.

I sat there thinking over how I had ended up there.

I had received a call the week before, from *Richard C*, who had been given my name by the friend of a client.

Richard asked me if I would have a look at one of his racehorses, which was kept in the racing yard of a well- known trainer near the Epsom racecourse.
He briefly explained that the vet had diagnosed this horse, with a condition called *kissing spines*.
'Could you have a look at Swainson?'
'You come highly recommended', he said.

So I agreed to meet him at the yard of the famous trainer at Epsom.
That afternoon I found, after a last-minute cancellation by a client, to have around forty-five minutes of extra time on my hands.
So I called *Richard* and spoke to his answer phone, saying that I would be at the yard early, and was that okay?
Little did I know what awaited me there…

I arrived to find the racing yard deserted.
No one about.
Just horses poking their heads over their doors inquisitively.
As I was about to go back to my car, a groom came up the road, swinging a bag of provisions.

I told her who I was and whom I had come to see, and added that I was a little early.

She cheerfully waved me into the yard and suggested I wait there,

'Go and introduce yourself to Swainson ', she said.

So I did.

I went over to his stable (which was clearly marked with his name board),

Spoke to him and stroked his neck.

It was at this point that the quietness of the yard was shattered by the angry voice of the famous trainer…

So there you have it: I was banished from the yard, and after around fifteen minutes of my waiting in my car with a bruised ego, *Richard* arrived.

He was hugely apologetic when I told him of my unwelcome reception,

He seemed every inch a gentleman, everything the trainer was not!

We walked back into the yard, now more like a lion's den to my memory.

I was then formally introduced to the choleric trainer, whose response to *Richard's* mild rebuke around my rude reception was simply,

'You just don't know what sort of a day I've had!'

No apology.

'Well', I said, unable to contain myself, *'I haven't been spoken to like that since I was in the army!'*

No reply.

As we walked over to *Swainson's* stable the trainer fired question after question at me, all in the name of professional interest, of course.

'Is this Reiki that you do?'

'Is it acupressure'?

'Are you a fan of Monty Roberts?'

I replied affirmatively to one of these, to which he snorted:

'Load of rubbish, typical American!'

He also said that a healer had visited *Swainson*, and mentioned her name.

Oddly enough I had just read her book, as a client suggested I would find her approach very similar to my own.

She had cost them a lot of money, the trainer snorted, including the purchase of a special blanket, which she had recommended for his back...

Finally I was in the stable with *Swainson*, a very feisty young horse.

His rider was holding him, she was a very
experienced woman; who clearly was a little quizzical
herself.

Three pairs of eyes watched intently, no: four,
Swainson too!

The questions continued; I felt I was facing the Grand
Inquisition;

I mustered all the patience I could.

Richard seemed to intuitively understand my problem,
and managed to switch the trainer's attention to the
subject of racing.

With the trainer suitably distracted, I was now able to
focus entirely on the horse, finding some physical
issues of a specific nature.

I had come across horses with similar problems,
Namely, the so-called *'kissing spine syndrome'*

It was clear that this horse was really uncomfortable,
All the muscles along the spine were in a permanently
protective state of tension:

The spinal nerves were therefore continually irritated,
Even if he wanted to, there was no way this poor colt
could relax.

His action, his whole body was affected.

He needed a rest.

I took a moment to centre myself.

Expectant eyes scanned me,

Awaiting my verdict.

With confidence, knowing how much was expected of me,

I delivered my assessment:

'Swainson is in a lot of pain and discomfort.'

'The tense muscles in the spine are creating irritation to underlying nerves,'

'This irritation is, in turn, causing problems with co-ordination.'

'It may well be that he has been backed too soon, at too young an age.'

'He will need to be long reined, no rider for a time; and I will need to visit him weekly for at least three weeks, then we can assess whether he will need further sessions after that.'

'It will take time.'

'In the meantime, give him a bit of a rest.'

'I cannot guarantee that he will completely recover, we can only do our best'

To my surprise, everyone agreed with this assessment,

Including the trainer.

The work started.

I saw *Swainson* weekly for around three weeks, then about a month later.

Improvements were noticed:

He was better in himself, more relaxed and clearly in less pain.

Without the pressure of racing, and with no rider on his back,

He was far happier.

Sadly, at this time his owner, *Richard*, became very ill.

He had been bravely fighting a life-threatening disease for several years,

Now it was getting the better of him.

I have heard no further news of *Swainson*,

But his life, I am sure, is better.

Only later did I discover, through a mutual acquaintance, that the 'angry trainer' had been, the very day I first visited his yard, suspended by the Jockey Club for some infringement or other.

Hence the anger.

He needed to dump that anger on someone. I just happened to come along right then! It's all too easy to take things personally, to choose to take stuff on board:

That's the game the ego in all of us plays:

The constant game of point -scoring,

The endless game of one-upmanship.

But that's not what this book is about.

This book is about some of the horses I have worked with.

It's also about some of the people who work with those horses.

And it's also about my reactions, my experiences with all of them.

Sometimes one can be all too human in one's responses to situations.

It's easy enough to react,

Especially to the anger or negativity of another person.

I use the technique of *reminding myself that that person's anger or pain is coming from a place of being wounded:*

Attacking a wounded person is hardly going to solve their problem!

Compassion is the key.
For all people,
For all creatures,
For all of creation,
We are all connected.
What I do, think and feel affects me, you, everyone and everything else,
For we are all One.

Chapter Thirty-Three: *Major and Fern*

Two recent cases came up, and although the horse and mare involved have totally different issues, they are worth the mention since I go to the same yard to see them.

The first to be treated was *Major*, a horse respected for his show jumping prowess in the past. Now, however, he had developed lameness, according to his new owners, and had not been in work for some time. When I went to see him „*Jackie*, who shares him with *Karen*, met me.

The horse was led into the yard from a paddock he was sharing with a mare called *Fern*, about whom much will be mentioned later.

I placed my hands on *Major* and waited.

I did not have long to wait:
My immediate impression coming from him,
inwardly, was one of sadness;
Deep, deep sadness bordering on depression.

Why?

Because he had been kept off work.

For good reason of course, he had gone lame;

But this had created, in *Major's* mind, a sense of rejection,

He felt he was no longer needed..

I have covered this elsewhere in the book, and it is quite common.

Horses can and do feel rejected by their owners if they are suddenly kept off working for long periods of time.

On the other hand, they will often create illness, usually lameness, when they are not able to exert themselves, usually as a result of overwork.

Its all a question of balance, isn't it?

So there I was, picking up *Major's* depression.

In addition to this, there were a number of other problems.

I found a massive amount of accumulated tension in his spine,

Clearly there as a result of all the years of exertion, show jumping.

This was, in turn, bringing on the lameness.

What he was also saying to me was that *he wanted to be out in the field,* rather than being restricted to the paddock with the mare.

(I suspect they are not that compatible!)

At this time he was being kept in his stable during the day, and put out in the paddock at night with the mare.

Without a blanket.

(This was an experiment by *Karen*, an attempt to lose some of his excess weight)

I worked for a time, during that first session, on his Heart centre,

Trying to clear the negative energy around the perceived rejection.

Next, I brought my attention to his spine.

The wings showed themselves as being slack, grey and dull in colour,

This horse was losing his reason to live!

For a while I kept my hands on the withers (over the wings) and lower back.

Then I gently applied the *BSR technique*; to stimulate the release of those tightly splinted muscles, especially in the spine.

This would, with the cooperation of the horse's own healing dynamics,

Bring healing and harmony to the system.

I stepped away from *Major* after about twenty minutes,
His first session was over.

I advised *Karen* and *Jackie* to keep *Major* warm, and to allow him access to the field during the day.
I suggested that his recuperation would be slow and steady, but that, from his point of view, he definitely wanted to come back into work:
This is a horse who just loves his work!
I felt that six to eight weeks of regular treatment would do it.
We had to go slowly, not asking too much of him to start with.
What made things slightly difficult was that, in my view, too many things were being thrown at the problem by *Karen*, whose yard the horses are kept in.
She was experimenting with dowsing and homeopathy.
I aired my thoughts, tactfully of course, and suggested a follow up session the next week.

Karen looked a little dazed, and said, by way of explanation that she had 'picked up' the healing I had facilitated on *Major*.

She felt quite emotional, and in fact, it turned out that this would intensify over the next day or two; leading to insights on her part, over treatments in general.

Major continued, over the ensuing weeks, to improve, quite literally, in leaps and bounds!

At one point *Jackie* got a little over-eager and took *Major* out hunting.

This was not, in my opinion, a good idea, as he became hugely overexcited and overexerted himself.

This showed up during the course of his follow up session, as some strain on the musculature;

I advised *Jackie* to take things more steadily with him, suggesting that hunting would not do him any sort of good at that time.

She agreed, and *Major* has shown his recovery to be exponential.

Mostly, he now knows that he is valued, and that his work as an event horse is appreciated.

He is, to date, doing really well.

He has completely recovered from his depression, and enjoys life.

Next, I turned my attention to *Fern*, the mare.

First impressions were that this was a mare who was not at all comfortable with herself.

In what way?

Firstly, there were issues around her gut.

I sensed ongoing problems there, and *Karen* confirmed this.

She said she had been addressing that area for some time, trying to approach the gut as holistically as possible, using homeopathy and herbs.

Next, I 'saw' a reddish brown foal, standing by *Fern*, as clear as day!

Was it coming from her past or her future?

Hard to tell.

Clearly though, it was there for a reason.

Could it mean that the mare had this foal taken from her?

Or could it mean that having a foal would be a good thing, would help with the hormonal system?

Information of this kind does not always appear to be useful or relevant,

But who am I to question Spirit?

251

Like the information I received from an Icelandic pony I treated some years ago:

He told me, clearly and unambiguously, *that he had seen badgers in the field the night before. Not only that, but he wanted me to pass this information on to his owners!*

I did.

They laughed, but confirmed that it was likely to be true, since he was often seen staring out into the dark late at night!

Why was this information relevant?

Did it make the people at that yard more believing, more receptive?

Possibly.

Did it make the pony happier to know he was being listened to?

Definitely!

I digress.

Fern, with the second visit, again presented the image of the little foal to me, as if this information really needed to be accepted and if possible, understood!

I can see it right now:

The foal is reddish brown in colour, with a white stripe down the front of its head: altogether a very pretty little thing.

With this second session also came new insight into her diet.
I saw a sticky brown mass: the image seemed to suggest sugar, that sugar would not be a good thing for her.
I mentioned this to *Karen*, who confirmed that she had picked this up herself, through dowsing. She felt that the mare may have been given some 'nuts' while she was away on holiday, and that these little treats definitely contain sugar.

Fern has since been given aloe vera as a supplement to help the gut lining,
We hope she will eventually recover from this particular problem.
As to the foal, the future will reveal all!

These two horses, *Fern and Major*, demonstrate once again the importance of appropriate action.
They also demonstrate the healing power of love,
Its harmonising ability in all things,

In all situations, regardless of the particular malady or condition.

I mean this in a way which transcends sentimentality,
The simple crooning of sweet words or petting and stroking of an animal.

This would only be a mirror for the love of the owner towards himself or herself.

True love for an animal not only breaks down the barriers to understanding,

It brings in a harmony of souls, and a healing power greater that we are usually aware of.

Let me say this again:
I am only a facilitator for healing to occur:
The real power of healing comes from somewhere else,
From All That Is,
From the Beyondness.
We feel this power as Love,
This raises us to a higher awareness of our selves and all of Nature.
This is what makes us special, the knowing that this power is within us,
Is indwelling.

Chapter Thirty-Four: *Moet*

You know how some horses just make you want to
cuddle them immediately?
I am sure you do.
These are the special ones, who have been sent to
show us how to love,
These are the angels of the animal kingdom.
And they will love us, all of us, whoever we are,
whatever we have done.
Perhaps they are emissaries of love, come to teach us
about unconditional love?

Whatever they are, I am going to mention *Moet*,
Who is one of these very special, very loving beings.
I met this very effervescent thoroughbred some nine
years ago, whilst visiting a yard at *Hilders Farm in
Edenbridge, Kent.*
This was a very formative time in my early contact
with horses.

It was also where I met some of the people who have shaped and guided my career in the field.

Amongst those is *Shelagh B*, the loving owner of *Moet*.

She is a very intuitive person, very trusting of those subtle intuitive energies; and I felt wonderfully connected, wonderfully confident with her support at that time.

(Thank you, *Shelagh!*)

Also a great support to me at that time was the owner of *Hilders Farm, Sarah W*, a very well known teacher and former Olympian horsewoman.

Sarah is considered formidable and an excellent and respected teacher, and back then I treated a number of her horses.

This sounds like name-dropping, and it probably is, nevertheless, these people were formative, and certainly deserve mention for the respect they brought to my work, not to mention the referrals.

So here I was with *Moet*, this friendly and loving horse.

From the first, he showed a willingness and intelligence in equal measure.

There is with *Moet* a decidedly telepathic rapport, which makes my work so much easier.

When I put my hands on him, I found an immediate response.

He lowered his head, allowing the energies to flow through him.

So marvellously expressive was *Moet*, he would yawn and stretch himself, as if to say:

'Look everyone, it's obvious that something good is happening to me!'

'Just see how I'm responding!'

Sure enough, *Shelagh* reported back to me that *Moet* had shown a positive response almost straight off: he felt better, moved better, gave more.

The news spread, *Shelagh* is a dedicated rider and knows a lot of people.

Even today, I continue to pick up referrals through her (and *Moet*, of course!)

When I see *Moet* from time to time, I can tell he remembers me at once,

He is affectionate and loving to such a degree that I wonder who is healing whom!

This is another fact of my work:

It makes me feel good!

It's not glamorous, and it's not always easy, but it makes me feel good!

What could be wrong with that?

Chapter Thirty-Five: *Pepper*

This was by far the biggest horse I had ever treated.

He was so tall, I found myself having to stretch my arms and hands upwards to reach his back.

He was also a bit intimidating.

Being in the stable with him made him as nervous as me, it seemed; not a good combination!

Clearly, this was a horse who did not know his own strength and power.

He did not even realize just how enormous he was. He was as jittery as a lamb, a small person in a giant's body!

Rebekah, his owner, had called me in to have a look at him.

It was obvious that she loved him to bits, their bond was clear to see.

His past had definitely left *Pepper* emotionally scarred.

I danced around in the sawdust with him,

Talking softly, trying to keep him (and myself) calm.
After only a few minutes of contact, I left the stable.
This felt appropriate, and as I have mentioned before
in this book, it is often a good idea to take things
slowly with nervous horses.

I told *Rebekah* that there were a number of areas in
which I could offer help to this giant of a horse.
In addition to the emotional scarring, which would
have to be addressed,
I found that *Pepper* had some specific areas of tight,
protective muscle.
This was causing additional discomfort and eroding
his self-confidence.
I made an appointment to see him the following week.

What a difference!
I could now stand with *Pepper*, in his stable, without
him feeling that he needed to move away from me.
He stood still, relaxed and attentive.
I worked very gently over his spine, feeling for the
areas where muscles had tightened protectively.
I had already decided that I would allow *Pepper* to
show me where his comfort limits were and I would
proceed only at a pace that was not invasive to him.

I needed to win his trust, to build a relationship on that.

People had misunderstood this horse all through his life, believing that, due to his sheer size, he would need a firm hand.

Inside, he was small and scared.

He had become used to being handled roughly, mostly by people who felt intimidated by his sheer size!

These are the usual misunderstandings generated by fear.

As a result of these misunderstandings, *Pepper* was seen as difficult and unpredictable, even dangerous…

Rebekah , through her love of the big horse, had seen through his defensive behaviour and was able to forge a bond of trust.

I should add something else, and that is that I had treated *Pepper* before, when he was stabled elsewhere, with a different owner.

Because her approach was less sympathetic than *Rebekah's*, not as connected, the horse had not prospered there, and was seen as wilful and dangerous.

Which in fact he was at that time!

If I had not been told, I truly would not have recognized him as the same horse.

So here I was seeing, intuitively, a baby inside a huge body!

The baby would throw a tantrum when he became upset, but the baby would also respond to gentle words of encouragement and love.

A pattern of the emotional scarring began to emerge: As soon as he was put under too much pressure during an event, *Pepper* would back off, shut down.

Effectively giving up on himself.

This was a confidence issue, or rather, a lack of confidence.

What we decided was that he needed constant rewarding.

Every time he got it right, he was fussed over, rewarded emotionally.

This became a new process, a new learning system for him.

Clearly the old system did not work for him,

He was too sensitive to be forcefully bullied into cooperating: he would just run away, even shut down.

This pattern displayed itself during show jumping,
when he would simply stop,
refusing to attempt the jump.

So, after a few weeks of treatment, a different horse
began to emerge.
This was a happier horse, one who was gaining
confidence in his abilities, his strength.
He was responding to a new approach, one that had to
do with encouragement, where he was rewarded for
his efforts and shown a loving response.
He thrived.
Rebekah found him more affectionate, more willing to
take chances.

The areas of tight, protective muscle gradually
released, making for better coordination and
movement.
As *Pepper* felt more comfortable in his body, so he
felt more able to do enthusiastically what was asked
of him, and more besides.
I saw him over a period of some weeks, gradually
extending the intervals between treatments, as we
noticed improvements.

As with all cases, 'fine tuning' occurs over time, gradually less and less effort is required to bring about balance, wholeness, and wellness.

Pepper is now enjoying his life, and that's the way it was always meant to be,
Wasn't it?

Chapter Thirty-Six: *Fire damage*

One very recent visit to a familiar yard led to a puzzling case.

A chestnut mare called *Minke* was presented to me, and I was immediately overcome, standing by her in her stable, by a sense of panic coming from her.

The mare was showing the whites of her eyes, something she apparently routinely exhibited.

But it was more than just the way she looked: Everything about her showed the after-effects of a traumatic event.

She would cooperate with me for a few brief minutes, then break away to circle the stable, barging away all in her path.

There was no apparent trust or respect shown for humans, as far as I could see from *Minke's* behaviour.

What had caused her to display such anxiety?

What had led to her having to be this defensive?

Little was known about her earlier life, but she has a beautiful shape and conformation. I could see, with that first visit, that the mare had a lot of potential.

 After my first session with her, which I found very tiring (some treatments can feel that way, especially with an anxious horse), I came away with very little in the way of an explanation for her state.
When I visited her the second time, I was told that she had slept almost continually for around four days following my visit!
Interesting!
This was going to be quite a session, I could just feel it.
Minke proved to be so restless and unable to settle down, that I decided, on a suggestion from *Cheryl*, her minder, to treat her outside the stable, on the concrete forecourt.
This would also allow her to feel that she could get away if she needed to.

Immediately I put my hands on her I again felt the sense of panic in her.

I stayed with it, with her, even though she was becoming dangerously anxious, rolling the whites of her eyes, shifting about nervously.

Before my mind, in complete clarity, I could see a fire, a big fire.
This, for a horse, is just about the most primal fear there is:
Fire.
I stayed with the mare, speaking softly to her to calm her down.
At the same moment I '*became her*', staying there with that sense of panic.

I could feel deep emotion welling up inside.
The conflict in her;
Having to resist her first instincts to panic and run away.
Instead, I got the sense that she was being held there, against her will.
Why?
I don't know, that part was not available to me.
On a whim, I decided to include some energy tapping in the healing.

I became a surrogate for her, making myself *Minke*
and tapping out the fear, the panic.

The response in the mare was immediate:
Suddenly she relaxed, her head dropped, her eyes
closed!
At the same moment I felt a rush of energy, the sense
that a part of her had returned to her, the part that had
stayed trapped by the fire.

This was remarkable.
I have never had a case like it.
There was the definite, inescapable feeling that I had
gone to some place of fear and trauma, returning from
it with a part of this horse's soul that had been held
there.
Soul retrieval?
Certainly it is my version of whatever that might
mean.
It brought home to me that I have probably been
doing work of a similar kind for some time; with
many or most of the animals I have treated.
I had not been able to explain or articulate the
experience till now, with *Minke*.

Clearly then, she had been traumatised by being restrained from her instincts to flee the fire.

This had then led to her distrust for humans.

How could she possibly trust or respect a species that would force her to stay with something so terrifying and destructive, against which she had no defence, but to flee?

This had then created a lifetime of constant anxiety, even panic.

What would they make her do next?

One cannot imagine what other thoughts were circulating in this poor mare's head. Certainly she was not well disposed to human beings.

A few days after that session, *Cheryl* informed me that *Minke* was so much improved; she was now 'almost affectionate'!

This was not in her vocabulary a week before.

Of course, *Minke* will need more help, but I believe the essential healing has been done:

She has been given back to herself, her soul has been returned to her.

Gradually now, she will begin to trust humans. With *Cheryl* and *June* she is assured of the best possible care. Their application of the *Monty Roberts* technique of '*Join up*' will be an important part of that rehabilitation.

Mostly though, she will need plenty of reassurance and loving-kindness.

Everything will grow from this new point of trust.

Chapter Thirty-Seven: *Conclusion.*

By now, with over fifty case histories described, I
hope I have given you, the reader, some idea of the
work I do with horses.

Also, although it was never my intention to write a
'how to' book, something may well result from the
reading of these pages.

Who knows?

It may well be that a reader, in the early stages of
learning to use the powers of Intuition and intuitive
healing, is encouraged by these descriptions.

Better still, that such a reader decides to enlist the help
of an Intuitive to help a horse, particularly when
conventional treatments bring no response.

Certainly, I have had dealings with some very
intuitive horse owners over the past ten years; people
who have learned to trust these 'special feelings'.

Some of these people have been mentioned, but if
they have not, I heartily apologise for their omission.

I realize, in writing the book, just how much I enjoy this work. How much I look forward to my visits to all the stable yards.

The atmosphere of these places is always rich with the busy comings and goings of horses and riders.

When there is time for it, there are stories over cups of tea; how this event went last weekend, how this or that horse fared, how well or how badly, and especially; how comfortable the horse and rider were after some healing work.

Just listening, at such times, has brought much to me in the way of learning, about both species: horse and person.

It is wonderful to see, to hear, just how much things can change for the better in this often-delicate partnership.

What I think it comes down to is this:

Your horse, dear reader, is always willing to listen to you. Even if it is not willing, it is always listening.

But, are you listening to your horse?

Are you aware of what it is trying to tell you?

Perhaps a sore back is the cause of that bucking,

That stiffness as you lead the horse out.

Perhaps a trauma from the past is creating those behavioural problems,

That lack of trust, that sudden fear as you canter
away through the woods.
That reluctance to take a bit in the mouth…

Your horse is telling you, with every move, with every
shift,
Are you listening to your horse?
Are you listening to yourself?

I do not intend to preach, to proselytize,
Only to offer an alternative to the current
predominance of the use of force to dominate this
willing creature, for that is what it is: willing, and
more besides; intelligent, patient, forgiving.
Endlessly forgiving.

I use an Intuitive approach to my work.
With this approach, or attitude, I combine (depending
on what is appropriate) hands-on healing with
intuitive healing; as described in the preceding
chapters.
In applying this, there is no force, no violence.

It is not always possible to elucidate with any real accuracy what it is that is being applied, less so, questions like:

How does it work?

Why does it work?

On what level is the healing occurring?

What is it that you do?

What do you call yourself?

These are questions I have tried to answer, inasmuch as I have the answers or am able to supply them.

But some things cannot be explained.

Some things don't need to be explained.

And I certainly don't have the answers to everything.

In the attempt to explain the details of the how or why, the actual living energy of that healing, the active force of *love* can be overlooked or ignored.

It usually is.

The real facts are:

Love heals,

Love makes whole what has been divided,

Love allows us to see the bigger picture.

Again, the word *love* is not used sentimentally. The context here is not here limited to just human feelings or an outpouring of affection.

It is a process, an Intention, a deliberate raising of energy; an attempt to reconnect with *Source*.

In doing that, there is the recognition of a higher state of Being, a realization, on my part, that I am merely a facilitator, a conduit through which energy flows or reconnects.

I step away from believing that I am the source of that energy.

I step away from seeing myself as that which effects the Healing.

I step away from taking the credit for a miracle.

Love is the source.

Love effects the Healing.

Love makes the miracle.